NATURAL WINE, NO DRAMA

NATURAL WINE, NO DRAMA

an unpretentious guide

Honey Spencer

PAVILION

We are drunk on the essence
without even tasting the wine,

Filled with light in the morning,
and joyful into the night.

They say our path leads nowhere –
that's alright:

There's joy enough right here to fill all time.

RUMI

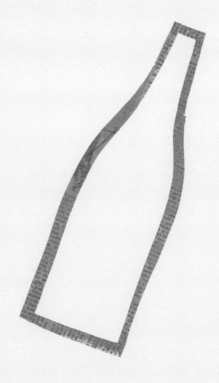

For my mother Angela Bionica

A NOTE FROM THE AUTHOR

I spent a decade trying to convince people to drink natural wine. I tried every angle. There was (naturally) the ethical argument: *Do you really want to be responsible for supporting an industry that is sending the planet into climate oblivion?*, I would nag. Then the gastronomic angle: *But! Consider! Natural wine offers so many more dimensions of flavour and texture than conventional wine. Conventional wine is predictable! Don't you want the wild, the beguiling, the unknown?*, I would shout into the void (or across the table to any of my guests who would listen). But, for so many years, natural wine remained staunchly alternative, a fringe movement, a sub-culture. And for what it's worth, I was happy to play my part as a sort of hipster pied piper.

Then the pandemic happened, and things moved more quickly than I could have imagined. With global lockdowns came the (somewhat ironic) clamber for exploration and adventure. For many, this craving for freedom manifested itself through activities like buying expensive cycling shorts, dusting off recipe books, or, as in my case, drinking *a lot* of gin around 4.00pm.

But, what I also started to see quite quickly was large swathes of my friends and wider communities reaching into their 'cellars' (reads: yeah right, under-bed storage drawers) and glugging down the bottles they'd been saving for years for the 'right moment'. As for the friends with little or no wine in their fridge (also me by this stage), I noticed them heading to their local wine shop and stocking up. Sometimes several times a week. And instead of spending £10 ($12) on a bottle, spending £15 to £25 ($18 to $30). Then reading up on the wines, engaging with the winemakers on social media, savouring each new taste memory, each new nugget of information, each new interaction. All things none of us in the wine trade could have conceived of before 2020, and at lightning pace. Wine sellers thrived, and the curious swelled their knowledge, their palates (and dwindled their wallets).

At the same time, I saw a lot of brilliant people bravely stride into the sphere of natural wine from outside the wine world. Uninhibited and unafraid of the rules, hierarchy or judgement, they swooped in and made their mark, finding new creative ways of generating new audiences for wine. Suddenly, it seemed, everyone and their whippet were drinking natural wine. Drinking, *good* natural wine. And understanding it. Pairing it with interesting foods from around the world. Sharing it, forging communities, and their own stories, making plans to visit vineyards when life got back to normal. I had long argued that natural wine is for everyone, and finally it seemed, it was.

an introduction to
NATURAL WINE

IT'S ONLY NATURAL

I still remember the first time I tried a 'natural' wine; I recall it with a shudder. It's a tale I seldomly tell because of the direction my life took swiftly thereafter. The year was 2011 and I was a freshly qualified sommelier on a second date with the flirty lad from work...

We ordered two glasses of Merlot at a new wine bar in Soho. The taste is familiar; comforting; a cascade of black brambly fruits gives way to a pinch of white pepper. Job done; I sink into my smugness. The date is going well: two more glasses, please. The waiter tops us up. But what is this? A taut wine, a slight fizz, spiky little red fruits. I jolt. Surely this is a different wine. The waiter assures me it is the same. She tells me we had the last two glasses from the previous bottle, and this is a fresh bottle. The wine behaves differently sometimes. *'This is a natural wine,'* she declares. *'But how on earth do you describe it to your guests?'* I retort, stung, as though the very grapes had been grown to offend me and now threatened to derail my date with the flirty lad from work.

I didn't hear the answer; I wasn't listening. Until that moment, wine and understanding wine had been a delicious formula to follow. Roses and a whiff of tar, well that must be Nebbiolo from Piedmont; buttery brioche and lemons left in the sun, Californian Chardonnay, no doubt. But this style of wine – ever-changing, enigmatic, with almost frustratingly human traits – I couldn't get it out of my head, and I couldn't make sense of it. I bought organic food whenever my bank balance allowed; I enjoyed pickled, ferment-y foods. I went to insect-eating pop-ups, I dated weird people I couldn't quite figure out.

Eventually, the flirty guy from work and I got hitched, quit our jobs and went travelling. London was filling up with this so-called natural wine, and yet I couldn't find anyone who could actually explain what on earth it was or how to work with it. Natural wine was developing a bad rep in some corners of town; others were embracing it. I had tasted life-changing bottles with such bedazzling purity and life that I couldn't imagine drinking anything else again. Other bottles were too sour, too funky, and smelled too much like my grandad's farm. Sommeliers were divided; the Baby Boomers were scared. We quit London and went straight to the source: Copenhagen.

There, restaurant noma was the gastronomic talk of the universe, and they were pouring exclusively natural wine to the most cultured and well-watered guests on the planet. And getting away with it. Out of bafflement more than anything else, I threw myself in. I ran natural-wine bars, worked for natural-wine importers, unloaded crates of natural wine from sail-powered ships, travelled with noma and my husband (who had scored a job there), to Australia, and then to Mexico. I worked as an intern in natural wineries in Adelaide, the Loire Valley, and then the Western Cape. I talked on panels and was interviewed for glossy magazines. Everyone, it seemed, wanted to know the secret to natural wine. I wondered what was happening back in London.

When I returned to London five years later, in 2020, I presumed nothing had changed. I would walk back through the wardrobe door, and the natural-wine Narnia would still be at odds with the rest of the world – and the boomers would still be cowering at the thought of a cloudy bottle. But how wrong I was. London, its sommeliers, and its drinkers, had grown up. At the time of writing, it seems we are approaching a sort of vinous summit. Sure, there are still bottles that give off a slight sparkle when opened, but servers are ready, and they prepare their guests for the phenomenon, showing how exactly to swirl the wine to lift any undesired effervescence, or bottles are lovingly decanted. But, more often than not, drinkers are up for it – they enjoy the unusual, the ephemeral, the human traits. They are no longer scared of sediment or haze, and winemakers are learning to leave their wines to settle a bit longer, so it's less of an issue anyway.

Last month, a lady in her sixties came into The Mulwray and ordered three bottles of £80 ($97) orange wine off the bat. *'Mum just loves it,'* her son beamed at me. A gentleman and his daughter ordered a bottle of *qvevri* wine from Georgia when visiting Evelyn's Table. *'It's a little … wild,'* I prepare them. *'Perfect, we love wild,'* replies the father. I get out my corkscrew and sink into a new kind of smugness.

NATURAL WINE, NO JARGON

It's easy to see why wine is often viewed as a total minefield – the terminology with which it is shrouded doesn't do much to make most wine-lovers feel at ease. Wine is a delicious beverage made by mostly uncomplicated and good-natured people, and it has always irked me how overly complex it has become. This glossary contains terms specific to the world of wine, particularly natural wine – feel free to use this as a reference to return to while flicking through the pages of this book.

Additives
There are over a few hundred tweaks/additions that can be made during the winemaking process. Extra sugar, acid, tannin, colour... you name it, may be added.

Amber wine
Aka orange or skin-contact wine. The OG – the earliest documented wine, discovered in clay vessels around 8AD – was an amber wine.

Ambient
Ambient or natural yeasts may be found in wineries or on the skins of grapes, and are used for kick-starting fermentation instead of using laboratory-made versions.

Amphora
A type of fermentation/ageing vessel made from clay. Many different shapes and sizes exist including egg-shaped terracotta *qvevri* from Georgia.

Balance
The 'holy grail' of harmony in a wine. Deeply subjective, but in general the impression of integration between the elements present in a wine (acid, fruit, texture), or feeling of 'completeness' in the glass.

Biodynamic
A farming theory invented by Austrian scientist Rudolf Steiner in 1924. The biodynamic calendar was later created by Maria Thun.

Brettanomyces

A type of yeast which creates a microbiological reaction in certain wines, resulting in deeply earthy, rural-esque aromas in the final wine. Commonly found in wines such as Châteauneuf-du-Pape.

Conventional

A farming model linked to the post-war and modern-day eras, which uses chemical agents such as fertilizers, pesticides, fungicides and herbicides to ensure high yields and mass production of grapes and wine.

Cover crops

Plants and vegetation planted in vineyards to encourage microbial life, and/or to help soil retain moisture and add organic matter to the soil and reduce soil erosion.

Crown cap

Aka a beer-bottle cap. Often used as a closure to seal in the bubbles on bottles of ancestral-method and pét-nat wines.

Decanting

The act of transferring a liquid into a second vessel. Commonly used in the serving of natural wine to encourage aeration and general integration of a wine.

Disgorgement

The process of removing dead yeast cells from a sparkling wine. Choosing to disgorge will often determine if a wine is clear or cloudy.

Dosage

The amount of sugar (in grams per litre) added to Champagne-method wines before bottling. Sugar is added to 'soften' the mouthfeel. Non-dosé = no sugar added.

Earthy

Popular term to describe natural wines that have a raw or rustic quality about them. Specific to aromas, flavours, or texture.

Élevage

Time spent ageing in either vessel (tank, amphora, cement, barrel) or bottle before the wine is released or consumed.

Faults

A chemical or microbiological flaw in a wine that is perceived as unpleasant by the taster or drinker. Some faults (cork taint) are more absolute than others.

Flor

A layer of yeast that naturally forms on top of wine in barrels that have not been topped up. Used in natural winemaking to prevent or slow down the oxidative process. Winemaking under flor often confers an interesting secondary nutty and spicy flavour to the wine.

Gamey

Popular verbiage for meaty or animal characteristics in wine.

Glou–Glou

The idea of a wine being 'gluggable', easy to drink, ephemeral, often light-bodied without significant tannin or structure.

Glyphosate

A type of pesticide/weed killer that is commonly used both in agricultural farming and homes for controlling weeds.

Hybrids

A grape plant born by crossing two or more different species of vine. Used increasingly to create disease-resistant varieties or ones that will adapt best to climate change.

Indigenous/native varieties

Varieties that are grown in the place they originated, for example Rkatsiteli from Georgia.

International varieties

This technically means the most widely planted grape varieties in the major wine producing countries in the world. Popular examples include Cabernet Sauvignon, Sauvignon Blanc, Chardonnay, Merlot.

Lees

Expired yeast cells left over by the fermentation process.

Maceration

Encouraging interaction between skins, stems, pips, and pulp of a grape resulting in extraction, structure, and tannin in a wine.

Malolactic conversion

A bacterial conversion of tart malic acid into creamy lactic acid, which always (and naturally) takes place in red wines, and sometimes in whites, where it can be encouraged or inhibited accordingly.

Massale selection

The practice of replanting vineyards from multiple cuttings of exceptional vines, rather than the purchase of single clones.

Microclimate

Highly specific weather conditions affecting vines that may pertain from anything from a tiny vineyard block to a small region of a few square kilometres.

Minerality

A textural or flavour sensation akin to crushed minerals, for example flint or wet stone.

Mousiness

A bacterial imbalance in a wine, most commonly associated with zero-sulphites winemaking. Said to remind the taster of licking a dead mouse.

Must

Grape juice before it is fermented.

Natty

A broad-reaching term referring to all things natural wine, as well as a specific unprocessed flavour profile.

Natural wine

Wine made without any additions or subtractions. Wine made as close to nature as possible.

Natural/indigenous yeasts

Aka ambient yeasts. Naturally occurring yeasts as opposed to specifically formulated versions designed for winemaking.

Orange wine

Aka amber or skin-contact wine. White wine made like a red wine; where the skins from notionally 'white varieties' are macerated with grape skins (and occasionally stems) to make a wine with greater colour and texture.

Organic

A farming and overall production method focused on the avoidance of chemical use in a vineyard and/ or winery.

Oxidation

The process of a wine interacting with oxygen. Can be positive (oxidative) or negative (oxidized).

Pét-nat

An abbreviation of the French *pétillant naturel*. A type of sparkling wine that undergoes just one fermentation, has no additions, and is finished in bottle.

Phylloxera

A rather nasty vine bug that ran riot around most of the world's vineyards in the mid-to-late nineteenth century. Certain key areas were spared, but all other vines had to be re-grafted to American rootstock, which is resistant to the pest.

pH (soil)

Scale to show how acidic or alkaline the topsoils are in a vineyard.

Pied de cuve

A native yeast culture made by fermenting grapes. This is then used to inoculate or help the main fermentation of grapes (similar to a sourdough culture).

Pipette
A piece of kit used in the winery to transport a small amount of liquid, often for the purposes of tasting wine from a barrel. Also known as a 'wine thief'.

PPM
Parts per million – commonly used as a metric for sulphur content in a wine. Same as milligrams per litre.

Pruning
Preparing a vineyard for the coming year by removing redundant properties from each vine.

Qvevri
An ancient type of vessel native to the Caucasus, which has a signature egg shape and is often buried in the ground or under the floor of the winery.

Raw
A popular term to describe unprocessed/natural wine.

Reduction
The result of a wine made in an environment starved of oxygen, often in an inert vessel such as a steel tank. Symptoms can often include the smell of a freshly struck match or burnt rubber.

Ropiness
Viscosity or gluiness apparent in wine when certain lactic bacterial compounds are formed.

Sans soufre (ajouté)
No added sulphites in the winemaking process.

Sediment
Spent yeast cells that are present in the bottom of a vessel or bottle and have a chalky or rocky-like appearance.

Soif
Aka Glou-Glou. Describing a simple refreshing easy-drinking wine for quenching thirst.

Solera
Otherwise known as a perpetual wine reserve. A barrel that is added to over several years so that the age of the wine is constantly and gradually increasing.

Sulphites
A naturally formed by-product of the winemaking process, sulphites can also be added to wine during winemaking as an anti-oxidant, antiseptic, and preservative.

Terroir
A unique combination of a vineyard's geographical location, soil type, aspect, climate, elevation, and other factors.

Typicity
The degree to which a wine reflects its origins (terroir or variety).

Umami
Aka the fifth taste. An earthy, salty richness present in foods such as MSG, mushroom, pork, sun-dried tomatoes, Vegemite/Marmite. Often used to describe the savoury aspect of certain natural wines.

Vigneron
A French term (but also used universally) to describe a person who both grows the grapes and makes the wine.

Vitis vinifera
The most common vine species planted around the world.

Voile
Aka a veil of 'flor'. Yeast layer that develops on top of wine in a barrel and results in a nutty depth of flavour in wines such as sherry, or oxidative wines from the Jura, etc.

Volatile acidity
Also known as acetic acid – a compound found in certain wines that gives off smells such as nail varnish remover and paint thinner.

Wine-grower
The person responsible for growing the grapes. This can be the person that owns the vineyard, or the person that owns the vineyard and makes the wine (aka vigneron). In this book, 'wine-grower' will be used to describe all producers who grow their own grapes.

Yield
The amount of grapes a vine can produce. Often measured in hectolitres per hectare.

Zero zero
A wine that has had absolutely nothing added to it or subtracted from it. In essence the truest form of natural wine.

WHAT IS NATURAL?

I remember a time I thought all wine was natural. I'm hardly to blame for the assumption, given the onslaught of wholesome imagery of rolling vineyards full of wildlife wine-lovers are subject to. And then, of course, there is always the image of the benevolent grandpa figure in the softly faded waistcoat, hunched over and dappled in the faint, cool light of his winery performing some painstaking act by hand.

What, of course, no one wanted me to see was what I stumbled across when I visited a particular section of Australia's famous Barossa Valley: mile upon mile of stainless-steel tanks, each groaning under the weight of 700,000 litres of wine and stretching as far and high as the eye could see, like some Mad Max-esque futuristic landscape, devoid of any sign of anything that resembled life at all, let alone grandpa with the waistcoat.

I suppose this would be the right time to concede that there is no such thing, really, as natural wine. The fact that vines by their very nature are climber plants, born to grow up trees and far away from the poles and trellises we've lured them along today means that only true natural wine would occur from a wild boar accidentally trampling some fallen grapes at the foot of a tree in a forest.

If a grape falls in a forest, and no one is around to tread it, is it really wine? – is perhaps the joke we should all be propagating over a glass of pét-nat. Maybe this forms the genesis of why government-binding legal definitions have been slow to get off the ground, although bodies such as Triple A (mainly Italy) and Vin Méthode Nature in France have been laying much of the groundwork for potential future legislation.

Still, much of the wine community dismisses the term natural altogether, opting instead for terms like 'real wine', 'raw wine', 'minimal-' or 'low intervention'. But regardless of its labelling, the quest remains universally clear: wine without the shit, please and thank you.

Before we dig in to the how, why, and frankly *WTF?!* – it's important to highlight that there are two key separate stages in making wine:

First, there is the growing of the grapes, aka farming. In an ideal world, this would be carried out by the same person, duo or collective that makes the wine, but commercial realities in many regions and countries can make this difficult, particularly for winemakers who arrive in the industry without an inheritance of vines, land for planting, or in general pockets the depth of the Bermuda Triangle. This can often be worked around by forging relationships with wine-growers who share similar ethical priorities to ensure the grapes are grown with the same care and respect that the wine will be processed with later on.

The second part of the journey begins as the grapes are harvested from the vineyard and finishes when the wine is packaged up and sent off to its next destination.

STYLES OF WINEMAKING

One of the most common questions that crops up is how natural wine differs to other styles of wine. *Does natural mean organic, or biodynamic? What on earth does 'biodynamic' mean anyway? And isn't 'regenerative' just the corporate buzzword-du-jour?* The following pages delve into the realities of each practice, both from a wine-growing and winemaking perspective.

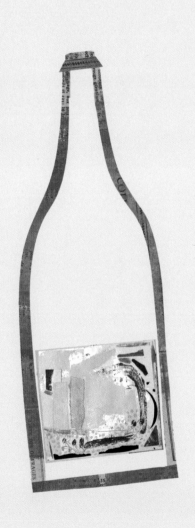

STYLES OF WINEMAKING

Conventional wine-growing

A term no farmer would likely shout from the rooftops, yet conventional farming is the go-to method of ninety-eight per cent of the world's wine-growers. A relative newcomer as an agricultural method (conventional farming only began as a method at the beginning of the twentieth century, against a backdrop of 10,000 years of growing vines domestically). Nevertheless, there are several reasons it has enjoyed Kardashian-esque success worldwide. At the core of the conventional method is the reality that a wine-grower has a vast lab kit of products to utilize as and when needed to boost grape yields, control pests, and generally reduce the amount of work that was historically required by hand in the vineyard.

In the middle of the last century, the Northern Rhône – an area infamous for its tough-to-work steep vineyard slopes – found itself in crisis. The effects of the Second World War saw many local men lost – the very same men who would have worked the difficult slopes and forge the region's heady Syrahs and viscous Viogniers. Without the farmers, no one could work the vines and the industry was on the brink of oblivion.

'After the war, natural winemaking wasn't just seen as anti-conformist, it was seen as anti-patriotic,' remembers Frank Balthazar of his eponymous domaine in the village of Cornas, during a visit in the spring of 2021. *'When the fertilizer salespeople turned up, the choice wasn't a hard one, the vineyards needed to be saved and these products offered a very real solution.'* And so, despite being invented in 1909 nearly half a century before, fertilizers were heralded as the saviour of much of European agriculture in the post war years, enabling bumper crops and nations' economies to restabilize. Pesticides – which involve a variety of compounds including herbicides, insecticides, fungicides, rodenticides, molluscicides, and nematicides – appeared to dramatically reduce the amount of work required in

the vineyard. Keen to maximize their recent recovery and swell their success, many of the world's winemakers started to use their new lab kits to shift from small-scale artisanal production to industrial levels, and the 'Chemical Revolution' was born (ironically, also called The Green Revolution).

However, it wasn't long before the cracks started to show. Wine-growers around the world soon began to find themselves in a vicious cycle, heavily reliant on the very products that promised them prosperity and freedom. Rivers were polluted from 'run off' from the vineyards, affecting the drinking water for miles around. The soil, once abundant in microbial life, was dead and lifeless. This presented a new challenge to the wine-grower.

'If you use herbicides then you need to use fertilizer. And if the roots can't feed off the soil then the concept of a terroir-driven wine is absurd,' says Nicolas Joly of Coulée de Serrant in the Loire.

The other challenge that remains today is the sheer amount of pesticides that are needed for wine-growing in comparison to other types of farming. Data shows that by the year 2000 vineyards comprised three per cent of France's farmed land, and yet accounted for twenty per cent of total national pesticide use, making grapes the most sprayed agricultural product alongside citrus fruits.

Conventional winemaking

Once in the winery, the options available to manipulate conventionally farmed grapes are fairly limitless. Further to my once naïve assumption that wine is made of mainly – well – grapes, I am confronted with the reality that wine made conventionally can have another sixty chemical substances and compounds added to it along with many other interventionist processes that allow a winemaker to nip and tuck, twist and tweak a wine into a final product. And that's just within EU legislation.

Is your wine not crisp enough? Add acid. Too acidic? Add potassium bicarbonate and de-acidify. Need more body in your wine? Add sugar. Is too alcoholic? Add water to bring it down. Need more structure? Put in some powdered tannin. Worried some rotten grapes got harvested, not carefully by hand but by the mechanical harvester, and threaten to spoil the lot? Don't worry, just add a large dose of sulphites into the juice to stabilize it, just to be sure. At this point, the argument is less about the impact of chemicals on the environment as to what is safe or desirable to put into our bodies.

In the 1960s, commercial yeast became available, allowing beer brewers and winemakers to further accelerate their product's commercial potential. No longer at the whim of the natural yeasts on the grape skins and in the winery to guide the grapes through fermentation, winemakers could now control exactly how and when the wine would ferment, even able to pre-select flavours in the final wine. In a world that craved stability and recovery from the scars of its recent past, it's easy to see why these new 'techno wines' – easily controllable, industrially scalable – were received so well.

Organic wine-growing

Organic farming is in reality how every piece of land globally was managed from the dawn of the Neolithic era that saw communities begin to grow their own food and 'farm' the land until relatively fairly recently – the first half of the twentieth century when conventional farming arrived on the scene. Farmers growing their crops would have limited influence on how a harvest turned out. Today, and since its official recognition as an agricultural model in the latter half of the twentieth century, organic wine-growing has evolved somewhat and focuses on the avoidance of synthetic chemicals in the vineyard. Synthetic chemical fertilizers, pesticides, insecticides, and fungicides are prohibited, however organic farming does allow for a limited application of copper and unlimited amounts of elemental sulphur to vines – these have been used for over one hundred years as an attempt to eradicate fungal issues in the vineyard. Today, just under seven per cent of vineyards globally are organic and seventy-three per cent of these can be found within Spain, Italy, and France.

A note on copper
Copper, in particular, has long been a hot topic as despite being safe in small doses (and a part of human chemistry – we need it to survive), it has been significantly over-applied to vineyards over the past decades. Applied to vines as a treatment to help ward off fungal diseases such as mildew, today the challenge is managing its build-up in vineyards – many contain levels sufficient to demolish vital microbial life, including mycelial networks, which of course we are increasingly aware play a bigger role in biological ecosystems than we may have once imagined. Too much copper in the soil of a vineyard is also responsible for copper toxicity which affects root system development and plant vigour. The other downside of excessive copper residue, as with all pesticides (see Conventional wine-growing and winemaking, pages 28–30), is that they often end up in the water supply, which means water needs to be treated. Needless to say, copper requires constant nuanced management if ecosystems affected by the past are to fully recover.

Organic winemaking

Moving into the winery is where the concept of organic wine *can* become a little – for lack of a better expression – hazy. While organically farmed grapes form the foundation of organic wine, the seemingly 'hands-off' approach in the vineyard can become more technical once the grapes reach the winery.

Under EU law, organic winemakers can still add numerous amounts of additives and make edits during the winemaking process. So, while the lab kit for nips and tucks is still available to winemakers making organic wine, it is somewhat restricted.

Here again it is important to highlight regional certification variances as some countries are far stricter with their regulations than others. In the US, wines that carry the label 'Organic Wine' must have no added sulphites (10mg per litre is the limit to account for a small amount of naturally occurring sulphites during fermentation). By contrast in the EU organic wines are permitted to contain 100mg per litre for red wines and 150mg per litre for whites and rosés.

Do organic wines taste different?
In theory, wine made from just organic grapes doesn't taste any different from grapes grown conventionally, although more often I have found that the fruit feels a little more lifted in these wines than their conventional counterparts. Beyond this, it really depends on what a winemaker chooses to do in the winery. How many of the permitted edits a winemaker chooses will dictate the final flavour and textural expression of a wine.

As with all organic farming, its existence and increasing re-adoption as a model can only be viewed as a force for good, enabling farmers to work within distinct (if regionally varying) parameters. I am personally grateful to not be subjected to a cocktail of pesticides every time I take a sip of organic wine, and I think it's safe to say that vineyards must be, too.

However, many would argue that the regeneration needed in many of the world's vineyards requires a more radical approach than merely abstaining from using synthetic chemicals. There is also the risk that many wine-growers are too reliant on government farming subsidies to stay loyal to the commitment to farm organically should a new conventional product be developed, and its use encouraged.

STYLES OF WINEMAKING

Planet-friendly farming

At the foundation of natural wine lies sincere and proper farming. Without this bedrock, it is practically impossible to make natural wine, as supportive and corrective winery practices are often required to balance out insufficiencies in the wine. If I had a euro for every time a natural winemaker said to me that wine is made in the vineyard, I'd likely be able to buy a big chunk of Burgundy myself. Despite the lack of a universal governing body for natural wine (unlike biodynamics, which has organizations such as Demeter and Biodyvin, and organics, which has a multitude of certifications depending on where you are in the world), it should be unequivocally agreed that organic farming is the minimum standard for wine-growing. Additionally, natural wine-growers often seek to go above and beyond. Some practise biodynamics, permaculture, agroforestry, and/or regenerative practices such as no-till, cover cropping, and rotational grazing. Practices such as these take into account the whole ecosystem of a vineyard, and look to establish vineyards that are as planet-friendly as possible.

Regenerative farming

'Regenerative', like the words 'sustainable' and 'green', is a term that seems on the brink of being almost entirely engulfed by corporates, and yet it's the only term that truly captures the ideal of healing something that has been broken. The term first appeared in the 1980s, a time when the effects of post-war intensive conventional farming must have started to kick in.

'The overall concept is one of the taking of something that has been damaged or misused, and then regenerating it: modern agriculture has depleted the life and functioning of the soil

and this is about farming in such a way as to restore it, make it healthy, to replenish what has been taken out, to encourage biodiversity, and get it functioning again. And into this we must add social capital, too. This is true sustainability.'
(Jamie Goode, *Regenerative Viticulture*)

The upside of regenerative farming is unlike the far vaguer sustainable and green, there is a programme of practices to adhere to and the means to implement them. Many companies have realized that they won't meet their net-zero targets without investing in specific environmental initiatives in a meaningful way and regenerative farming practices is one of these. In short, regenerative farming looks to balance agricultural output with the protection, preservation, and restoration of the world's land and soils. Regenerative farming also looks to rebuild the soil's organic carbon stores, allowing carbon to be sequestered to the levels that it once was before the Industrial Revolution.

The five key principles of regenerative farming are to minimize soil disturbance, maximize crop diversity, keep the soil covered, maintain root health, and livestock rotation. Again, regional nuances are vital to the success of the model, particularly when it comes to vineyards which are especially sensitive to the minutiae of influences that surround them. The no-till method is one that many wine-growers are starting to gravitate towards. Summarized by Masanobu Fukuoka's work and subsequent book *The One-Straw Revolution*, the method zones in on the need to not disrupt the upper layers of soil by ploughing, or tilling. The growing of cover crops, i.e. planting crops that help generate movement and oxygenation of the top soil, is also becoming increasingly practised to help breathe life into dying soils.

Regenerative farming models, regardless of nuanced variations, share essential common values. Processes that require large inputs of energy or raw materials should be avoided. Nutrient recycling is a big focus. Overall, the aim is to bring back health and vitality to the soils and encourage biodiversity. In short, to generate life over death.

Biodynamic wine-growing

Invented by Austrian philosopher and scientist Rudolf Steiner in the 1920s, biodynamics in fact pre-dates organics by a decade or two, although in practice organic farming has been around forever, while biodynamic turns only one-hundred-years old this year.

The first thing to say about biodynamics is it can be pretty hard to get your head around. For starters, the cosmos is mentioned *a lot*. So are terms such as dynamization and numbers like #501. I made the mistake of lamenting the apparent complexities of the model to my friend Stephanie Tscheppe from biodynamic wine-growers Gut Oggau in Austria's Burgenland. *'Honey,'* she threw back, *'our ability for higher thought is all that separates us from animals, so we must try and seek understanding, to seek the truth.'* Obviously, she's right, I sigh internally as I try and figure out a way of distilling cosmic activities down to something digestible for this book, and my unsuspecting guests back at the restaurants. Sonoma County's first biodynamic-certified producer Mike Benziger offers up a great intro. *'At its core, biodynamics is an energy management system.'*

The concept of biodynamics is everything on the planet is living and gives off some sort of energy. Biodynamic farming is the practice of managing those energies. When put like this, it seems a lot easier to understand why a holistic approach is required to restore biodiversity and replenish nutrients in the soil rather than the idea of a 'silver bullet' – the same kind of thinking, we could argue, that got us into this mess in the first place. But really, biodynamics is about getting elements of an ecosystem to talk to each other and restore their lost connections. It's also about driving energy back into the land. *'Biodynamics is a radical regenerative philosophy,'* Stephanie's husband, Eduard, tells me as we prepare the #500 preparation, essentially cow manure that has been buried in cow horns, and is now mixed with warm water, which we work into a vortex (to mimic the direction of the galaxy in the cosmos), then spray onto the base of the vines from tanks that we strap to our backs. *'Conventional farming is like force-feeding a vine instead of training it to search for food. A vine's roots are its nutrient larder, and if it is receiving no real substance from the soil, then what we have is zombie vines, and ultimately zombie wines,'* Eduard adds.

The compulsory elements of biodynamic certification centre on the application of #500 and #501, a horn-silica mix, also buried in cow horns over summer and designed to stimulate photosynthesis and influence aroma and flavour of fruit in a wine. But there are a lot of other optional elements, too, all part of a wine-grower's tool kit to help the vines align closer to the cosmos and forge wines with not just flavour, but surging with life and power. The six composts included in biodynamic theory include elements such as yarrow, dandelion, stinging nettle, oak bark, valerian, and chamomile, which biodynamic wine-growers believe super-charge the compost and help plants improve their circulation by inspiring them to seek nutrients.

The biodynamic calendar, devised by Maria Thun in 1962, extended Rudolf Steiner's work, focusing on the link between crop cycles and the astrological calendar and identifying the best times to carry out works on the soil and on the plants in agriculture in general according to the position of the moon in different constellations of the zodiac. The Plato elements of earth, wind, water, and fire, all have their counterparts in agriculture: Root, Flower, Leaf, and Fruit, respectively, which refer to the sidereal moon cycle. At Gut Oggau, as with many other biodynamic wine-growers I speak to, these key timings are adhered to as much as practically possible. The soil is primed to receive preparations on 'root days', when the information contained within the preparations are thought to be more powerfully received by the soil. Harvesting is done where possible on 'fruit days'.

Biodynamic winemaking

It's true that most biodynamic practices occur in the vineyard ahead of winemaking, however the Maria Thun biodynamic calendar helps guide crucial timings in the winery, too. At Gut Oggau, the aim is to only transfer the wine – including bottling – on 'fruit days', when the wine is seen to be the most expressive and representative of its true self.

Demeter, the most widely recognized biodynamic certifying body, helpfully lays out both 'aims' and 'standards' for each stage of the winemaking process. For example, hand-harvest of grapes is the aim, although machine harvesting is permitted in some regions, but not others such as Austria. The leftover pomace from the process must be returned to the vineyard to feed the soil. In the winery, the aim is that the grape should be allowed to ferment from the naturally occurring yeasts found on the grapes themselves and in the vineyard, although organic or biodynamic 'pied de cuve' or GMO-free commercial yeasts are permitted, but again not in all regions such as Austria where the movement began.

Of course, many biodynamic wine-growers try to go far beyond the standards set by organizations like Demeter, ultimately drawing them closer to the concept of true natural wine.

Natural winemaking

Natural wine-growing and making is perhaps the simplest of all wine-related philosophies, and yet by far the hardest to pull off for those attempting it. The overarching principle is 'nothing added, nothing taken away', or 'wines made from the grape, by the grape, and nothing but the grape' *(so help me, Bacchus...)*.

In the winery, a lot of natural winemaking comes down to the famously tricky art of holding one's nerve. There are the obvious interventions that need to be made. Some grapes will be straight-pressed before fermentation begins; others may be macerated with their skins, depending on the style of wine that they will become. Some grapes will need some time to macerate with their skins, others can be pressed off their skins before fermentation starts.

Natural wines ferment with 'natural' yeasts (yeasts that are present on the skins of the grapes or in the winery). The fermentation starts after the grapes have been trodden or pressed. Inoculating the grapes with lab-cultured yeasts is seen by most as diverting away from natural winemaking and a form of excessive interference.

After natural fermentation is complete, the wine may need to be moved once or twice, ideally by gravity. Malolactic conversion, often blocked in conventional white wines to retain a wine's crisp and fresh profile, is not prevented, allowing the wine to undergo the conversion if the conditions are favourable.

And then there is the question of time and the vessel the wine will wait in until the time is right for bottling. Clay, concrete, steel tanks, and old barrels are most commonly used. New barrels are used sparingly as they are seen to impact the flavour and overall character of the wine too much and mask its terroir. Some purists even consider old barrels a step too far, opting for vessels that impact less on flavour and texture.

Conventional winemaking tweaks such as acidification (the adding of acid), and chaptalization (the adding of sugar to boost a wine's alcohol and body), are also highly discouraged in natural winemaking. Conventional wines may be filtered and/or fined before bottling to clarify the wine and remove any unwanted particles. Almost all natural winemakers will eschew these techniques, opting to keep these elements in the wine to enhance texture and character. The addition of sulphites, often the most contentious issue in the natural-wine discussion, should be kept to a minimum. Most natural wine producers will avoid adding sulphites as a matter of course, but are not so dogmatic that they would allow the wine to spoil for doing so. The more hardline natural wine producers opt to add none whatsoever.

THE LAND OF

LOST VINEYARDS

We hurtle along the twisted mountain roads emerging from the city of Taormina. It's Christmas time, and festive lights hang suspended above the city streets. I'd come to see Mount Etna, but Luca has something better to show me: the lost vineyards of Taormina. The region is part of an ancient volcano range called the Arco Calabro, which pre-dates Etna and stretches from Messina to Calabria. They've been making wine for so long here they don't even call it natural wine; they've just always made it like this. Harvested by hand, the grapes are loaded into a small basket press, then a few small barrels. Nothing added, nothing taken away. *Certo.*

I lean my head out the car window; the 20°C (68°F) heat washes over me like a guilty pleasure. It shouldn't be this hot in Sicily at this time of year. The local *vigneri* are worried about an early bud burst next year. Climate chaos is here knocking on Sicily's door, too. Luca's blue Fiat twists and turns around the ever-thinning roads of the *campagna*. I try to remember if I've written a will. He pulls over regularly: *'ça-ça c'est terroir,'* (That! That's terroir.) he shouts effusively in his Quebecois Sicilian, pointing at the rock formations cleared who knows how many years ago to form this road. Granite, limestone, some schist around too, he says. It's all here; he's right. This is true terroir, and it is dazzling in its complexity. How do sommeliers like me not know about this place? In a world that feels published, plundered, and eternally posted from every angle on Instagram, I rejoice at the increasingly inhospitable terrain as we drive into Luca's geographical oblivion. It's a new meaning to the term 'off-grid' – surely only a handful of cars ever traverse this terrain every year.

I survey the intensifying landscape. The cloudless sky is broken only by grasses and cacti, palm and olive trees. There is no doubt that this is a fertile region for growing grapes, for growing anything, frankly. The distant clang of goat bells is the only noise here in December as we join a further dirt road and into the property of Salvatore 'Turi' Longo (aka *l'Ingegnere)* and his wife.

Turi, is a quaint Sicilian with cascading silver hair and an impertinent twinkle in his eye. *'I wasn't born in this valley; I'm not the son of a winemaker,'* he says as he welcomes us into his miniature cantina, built halfway up the valley. Every time I hear these proclamations, I know there is a serious graft at play here. I think of my friend Alexandre Bain in Pouilly-Fumé, who had to start from the beginning, too, always grafting, always in some way disenfranchised, always having to work harder than the others to prove his worth. *'It took twenty years for me to purchase the eleven properties that it would take to form my domaine,'* Turi continues; it was a long time in the making. Finally came the miniature cantina and two small cabins – one a single room that forms the kitchen, the second with a mezzanine bedroom and small living area.

The view is unbelievable. I've stood in countless vineyards but never seen anything like this. A hidden ancient volcano range, with fertile valleys and vineyards, planted carefully on the slopes, some of which only have a few rows of a variety. Nerello Cappuccio, Nerello Mascalese, Carricante, Inzolia, and a long-forgotten local variety called Epola. The wines we taste haven't finished fermenting, and they are laced with a naive and playful sweetness, seemingly oblivious to the impending winter and the journey they must embark on to become finished wine. I think then again about how wine has frustratingly human traits and must undergo a similar evolution, dependent on time and walking hard, sometimes treacherous, roads to become all that it is destined to be. The wines we taste are good, embedded with a deep-set mineral complexity that will only flourish further given time in barrel and alone with their thoughts.

Turi generously fills up two bottles for us to drink with lunch before we leave, taking time to point out the inherent haze in the bottles of the wine poured fresh from barrel, which he compares to two other clear bottles devoid of any haze standing on a nearby shelf. *'Given time, all becomes clear,'* I translate to myself from *l'Ingegnere's* closing words. Natural wine doesn't have to be cloudy to mean it's unfiltered. Sometimes all you need is extra time and the haze will lift on its own. I draw myself away and take a moment to macerate in this unexpected truth.

the people behind

NATURAL
WINE

NAMES
TO KNOW

Every revolution has its First Movers, and natural
wine is no exception. These are the names you
need to know to understand how natural wine has
arrived where it is today. An A–Z of those whose
passion and investment in natural wine in the last
forty years has helped shape what we sip and how
we sip it today.

Alice Feiring

A journalist, author, and global spokesperson for natural wines, Alice has dedicated her life's work to travelling the world and communicating the message of wines that are made traditionally and with respect. She has published six books, including *Naked Wine*, *For The Love of Wine*, and *Natural Wine for The People*; and launched the world's first natural-wine newsletter, The Feiring Line, in 2013.

Elisabetta Foradori

An Italian winemaker from the northern region of Alto-Adige, when Elisabetta was a young winemaker she defended her domaine against the mounting pressures to replace native varieties with more recognizable, global varieties. The *agricola* is now run by her children Myrtha, Emilio, and Theo.

Gang Of Four

A group of four winemakers from the Beaujolais were inspired by their mentor Jules Chauvet to prove that Beaujolais can be so much more than cheap, gluggable wine, providing a window to the region's terroir given the right practices. The original gang was Marcel Lapierre, Jean Foillard, Guy Breton, Jean-Paul Thévenet, with fifth member Yvon Métras joining later.

Jules Chauvet

Beaujolais grower, biochemist, winemaker and merchant, and rumoured to be one of the most formidable tasters of his time, Jules Chauvet, was able to convince many winemakers across France to adopt a more natural approach in their viticultural and winery practices. His fastidious dedication to science allowed him to eschew chemical use in his vineyards and cellar, and his work spread across France, and marked a new dawn for the wine industry whose practices were until that point focused on mass production and standardization.

Kermit Lynch, Denyse Louis and Joe Dressner

These legendary wine importers were instrumental in imbuing the West and East Coasts of the US with low-intervention wines. They recognized the importance of temperature-controlled shipping for the wines to retain their true character. Kermit Lynch originally coined the term 'Gang of Four' and wrote of his travels in *Adventures on the Wine Route*. Kermit's son Anthony, and Denyse and Joe's son Jules have now taken over.

Lalou Bize-Leroy

Somewhat a lone wolf in 1980s Burgundy, Lalou converted her whole domaine – which included many of the region's finest vineyard sites – to biodynamic in 1989. Later, she formed an alliance with fellow Burgundian wine-growers Jean-Claude Rateau, Emmanuel Giboulot, Dominique Derain, Anne-Claude Leflaive and Alain and Julien Guillot, who still meet twice a year to discuss biodynamic techniques and help newcomers learn.

Lydia and Claude Bourguignon

Iconic microbiologists and soil specialists, Lydia and Claude Bourguignon have travelled the world to work for clients who want to know more about their terroirs. In 1990, they revealed, through a study for the Institute National de la Recherche Agronomique (INRAE), that the average French vineyard had less microbiological activity than the Sahara Desert. This catapulted some of the biggest names in winemaking into action, working to reverse the damage caused to their soils through intensive chemical application. Now in their seventies, Lydia and Claude continue their work.

Maria Thun

German-born Maria is responsible for the creation of the biodynamic calendar, formed from the cosmic elements of Rudolf Steiner's lectures, and years of experiments observing the connection between cosmic forces and the growth of plants. *The Maria Thun Biodynamic Calendar* has been published for gardeners and farmers of all sorts of agriculture around the world for over sixty years. For wine-lovers, the When Wine Tastes Best App highlights good and bad days for drinking wine according to the cosmos.

Masanobu Fukuoka

Regenerative Japanese farmer and author of *The One-Straw Revolution*, Masanobu established a way of farming, also known as 'Do Nothing Farming', based on reduced working of the ground to increase soil health. His practices are increasingly used today to combat issues caused by soil compaction.

Nicolas Joly

Custodian of the ancient Coulée de Serrant, established by the Cisterian monks in 1130, Nicolas was a key figure in Wall Street before returning to the domaine in the Loire Valley's Savennières. After reading the works of Rudolf Steiner, he was inspired to adopt biodynamic agriculture, which led to his Renaissance des Appellations, now an international association of biodynamic wine-growers. His daughter Virginie now runs much of the estate.

Pascaline Lepeltier

Loire Valley native, Pascaline is one of the world's most revered sommeliers. She has curated some of the best wine lists in the world over the last twenty years – notably in France and New York City, highlighting the work of natural winemakers. She has also won a plenitude of awards, including France's Best Sommelier, and does so to showcase the importance of responsible agriculture to the wider cultural conscience.

Pierre Overnoy and Jacques Néauport

Now one of the most highly respected wine-growers in the world, Pierre met winemaker Jacques Néauport (a disciple of Jules Chauvet) while making conventional wine in Jura in the early part of his career. Jacques convinced him to try making wine without added sulphites and since 1986, not a single bottle of his wine has received any sulphites. His wines prove that with fastidious farming, and patient winemaking, natural wines can age for decades into the future. The domaine is now run by his protégé Emmanuel Houillon.

Rudolf Steiner

The godfather of biodynamics. A physicist who dipped his hand into farming via a series of lectures in 1924. He suggested a link between cosmic activities and agricultural practices, which went on to form the basis of biodynamics.

Stefano Bellotti

From Italy's famous Gavi region in Piedmont, Stefano was an early adopter of biodynamic agriculture, converting his estate, Cascina degli Ulivi, in 1984. He was also the Italian president of Renaissance des Appellations (see Nicolas Joly). He died in 2018, and his daughter Ilaria now runs the operation.

Tony Coturri

One of the real OGs in natural wine, Tony was making natural wine before it was, you know, #naturalwine. Another early adopter of biodynamics, Tony has been doing his thing on Sonoma Mountain in California for over forty years, and was seen as a radical for his regenerative ideas before the science arrived to back him up.

'SIR' DOUG WREGG

It's a moody midsummer's evening when I clock off work and stride hurriedly up to London's Primrose Hill to meet Doug Wregg, Sales and Marketing Director of Les Caves de Pyrene, the world-famous wine import company. It's been a long week, and my temperament is matching the weather – sticky, and contemplative. I'm not really in the mood for talking, but there is much to say and much to ask of the man who almost single-handedly put natural wine on the map in the UK over two decades ago.

Luckily for me, I find Doug exactly as I've come to know him over the last decade, bubbling over like a fermenting barrel, his peppy prose primed for bottling. And of course, there is wine to perk me up. We sit down on the grass, overlooking the London skyline, and Doug pulls from his bag the bottle he has brought along – something I requested in advance that he considers to have influenced his career to date. I silently scold myself for expecting some sort of eccentric, amber liquid instead of the crystalline white Doug pours into my glass. Clos des Vignes du Maynes 2020 by Julien Guillot, the legendary producer from Burgundy's Mâconnais. The wine tastes like liquid gold, salt-crusted with ripe fruit and the broadness of acidity that can only really be Chardonnay. So pure, so well behaved, I thought, and yet belying a presence of something youthfully visceral and entirely alive.

Doug raises his glass, peering up at it. *'Growing up my father used to love old, dusty red wines, Riojas and such,'* he squints into the sun. *'I always thought wine was decay. The romance of dying. I thought good equated to old, like respecting the wisdom of an old man with a beard, or something like that.'* I ask him what had changed his mind.

'We had taken Chris Galvin (of London's celebrated Galvin restaurants) to Paris to try and convince him to sell natural wines in his restaurants. It was a disaster, every wine we tried at every restaurant and bar had something wrong with it. It was early on in my time at Les Caves, and I thought, if this is natural wine, I'm not sure I'm up for it. On the way home, we stopped at a tiny bistro and had a bottle of Olivier Cousin Chardonnay. It wasn't necessarily good, or bad. It was strange. It got me thinking if this is wine, what had I been drinking up to this point? I was captivated. Then we tried a bottle of the Clos des Vignes du Maynes. Most white wine that I knew was buttery or toasty, or it had a rigid architecture or at least a block of flavour that could be viewed as tasty. But this, this was totally wild. It had this energy that ricocheted around my tastebuds. It was breathtaking.'

After an early career ferreting around West London restaurant cellars as a sommelier, Doug was on the hunt for his next step and met Eric Narioo, a wine importer who had set up Les Caves de Pyrene, a small import business specializing in 'a handful of growers from the Languedoc and Southwest France'. Doug joined the then three-strong team, but the early years weren't laced with the same soaring success that would come later.

This was all happening in the 1990s: it was the 'Bordeaux or bust' era, and no one wanted to know about anything outside of Bordeaux, Burgundy, or Champagne. *'And yet, here we were, this teeny amateur company knee-high to a Diam cork and all we had were these obscure wines from obscure appellations. In other words, we were utterly irrelevant. Back then natural wine wasn't even just a fringe movement, the concept barely existed anywhere. There were vignerons working organically and biodynamically, but no one was talking about additives or sulphites.'* (The world's first natural wine fair would be established half a decade later – La Dive – in 2001).

But, despite a miscellany of cultural and financial obstacles, over time Les Caves slowly began to flourish. Everything seemed to ramp up around 2008 with the opening of Terroirs – Les Caves' first bricks and mortar site tucked in a quiet street behind London's Shaftesbury Avenue. Terroirs was a passion project for Doug who had longed for a public space to *'eat the food I wanted to eat with the wines I wanted to drink.'*

In the kitchen was a young Ed Wilson, who would go on to be an icon in his own right with strong ties to the music scene, alongside his East London restaurant Brawn and coastal outpost Sargasso in Margate. *'People didn't know what a natural wine bar was,'* remembers Doug. *'Our first customer ordered two pints of lager, and the second ordered a bottle of New Zealand Sauvignon. It went on like this for a while. A guest would order a bottle of "Pinot Grigio" and our sommeliers would bring out our idea of a Pinot Grigio: a near fluorescent skin contact wine from Dario Prinčič on the Italian/Slovenian border. We'd serve it at cellar temperature (10°C/50°F above fridge temperature), and we'd decant it. The guests' eyes would widen in fear. "What the fuck is this?" they would bleat.'* This is never, ever going to work, Doug thought.

But the guests kept coming. On some days Terroirs heaved with 450 covers. And slowly an acceptance of the wines developed. *'There was another couple who ordered a bottle of Elena Pantaleoni's Ageno, a skin-contact Malvasia blend from Emilia-Romagna, which had again,*

Wine fair: Poster for Real Wine In The Vines 2023 (Hemel Hempstead, UK)

quite a violent magenta hue. Again, we served it at cellar temperature and decanted, as we knew that was the way the wine tastes its best. I saw the reaction start to happen. But then something extraordinary happened. The table next to them leaned over and said, "ah yes, this is what's called an orange wine, it's made with its skins which gives it the colour." The guest said, "oh, okay" and drank the bottle without blinking. We crossed the Rubicon over, and over again in those early days. The greatest victory came with a solo diner who rolled in wearing a pin-striped suit and ordered a bottle of Sébastien Riffault Sancerre. Those wines are wildly cloudy, with a dark coral colour, totally wackadoodle, they were even too much for me!' Doug titters. 'The guest looked at it, took a taste and gave a thumbs up. He drank the whole bottle by himself. Okay, we've arrived, there is hope for the world,' Doug concluded.

It's apparent that the natural-wine movement has come a long way since the early days. But then again, so has Doug. 'I guess I have gone from starry-eyed idealism to a form of pragmatism. Once upon a time there was a company worth diddly, accountable to no one, and everything was worth the risk; now we have the jobs of forty-plus people to think about.'

Doug has also in recent years become more involved in the buying side of the business, working with wine-growers in eleven countries. 'The pleasure of buying is being able to introduce and share what you have discovered with an audience in the hope and expectation that it will gain the same pleasure and sense of discovery that you did on first encountering the wine. However, you have to balance aesthetic delight (i.e. what I like) with commercial viability (will we ever sell it?). Today's exciting new discovery can become tomorrow's bin end. And, as the buyer, you must take responsibility for that. I learned that buying isn't just picking and bringing home beautiful flowers; you also have to constantly nurture them.'

As one might expect of an Oxford English Literature graduate, Doug recorded absolutely everything as it unfurled. 'Being self-taught, I am into demystifying what has been seen as an obscure subject, hopefully without oversimplifying it,' he offers. A blog was started at some point along the line, and at the time of writing Doug alone has written 1,000 entries. He wrote and published *The Real Alternative Wine Glossary*, and in 2018 (to mark the company's 30th birthday), Doug released his opus: *The History of An Unusual Wine Company in 10½ Chapters*, a touching, and wildly funny, memoir of Les Caves' adventures to date.

I get the feeling that nostalgia is something Doug is particularly fond of, as we watch the London skyline and open a second bottle of wine that Doug has packed *'just in case'*. His excited effervescence has softened now, as if a wine decanted, and he speaks in broad brushstrokes, casting his net into a sea of memories. *'You know back then people thought we were practically fundamentalists, as if we were being contrarian for the sake of it. Even the term "natural wine" seemed loaded. A lot of work goes into making it, but it's just wine, for goodness' sake.'*

I ask Doug what he considers natural wine to be outside of its immediate parameters. Doug pauses... *'Natural wine is a natural coalition between plant and man. People tend to over-intellectualize it, to make it about formulas, which for me defeats the point. When I drink it, I ask myself, does it taste like undiminished nature? You don't sense the heavy hand of the winemaker. It's the taste of being alive in liquid form.'*

It's getting late, and a chill pricks the London air. I ask Doug for his take on the future of Les Caves de Pyrene, and the natural wine movement as a whole. *'That it will be talked about less and less and be more and more a fact of life!'* he winks, *'and besides, why does everything have to have a beginning, a middle and an end?'* I smile to myself; he's not wrong.

'I should be thinking about retiring, but I'm not ready to hang up my trainers.

I'd love to teach more, I've got more books to write. I'm also still very ambitious for the company.'

I think back to his first comments and life and decay, and how Doug seems in almost every way like the wines he now loves to drink, a million miles away from dusty, but youthfully visceral, and entirely alive.

Wine to try: Aragonite Mâcon-Cruzille (Clos des Vignes du Maynes – Burgundy, France)

THE TERROIRIST – downing Dionysus

MELI LIGAS, KTIMA LIGAS

I first encountered the wines from Ktima Ligas during my first position as head sommelier at an ill-fated restaurant on the edge of London's banking district in 2017. The restaurant was designed around open-fire cooking, and the coarse, yet spirited, Xi-Ro 2016 – a blend of Xinomavro and Roditis from the Greek region of Pella near the border of North Macedonia – offered an engaging match to the flame-cooked dishes on the menu. My guests loved the refreshing alternative to the usual red-meat-accompanying culprits, and I relished finding a new discovery of my own. A few years later in 2019, wandering along the ancient limestone tunnels of La Dive Bouteille I met a smiling and unassuming Meli Ligas, who had taken over her father's domaine the year before. We bonded over sharing the name Honey (Meli means honey in Greek), and as I sampled the wines, each taste poured filled me with a little electric charge that left me short of breath. When we reached the 2018 Xi-Ro, the underpinning of the wine I'd poured a few years earlier remained intact, but the wines felt purer; more lifted. *'I'm searching for a lighter expression of Pella,'* Meli confided.

It was another few years again before I revisited the wines; by which time Meli's ambition for the winery was unmistakeable. *'What the hell was that?'*, my wine merchant friend Imogen demanded, as we sat around a dining table one frosty January evening in London. The wine we'd just tasted blind was still rallying around our palates, with such clarity and verve it was hard to think about or discuss much else. Rosehips, peonies, fresh cranberries, black pepper, and baked herbs were working up a crescendo on my tastebuds. I checked the bottle. Xi-Ro 2020. I made a vow to get to know Meli Ligas.

We catch up over a WhatsApp video call in mid-July 2023. It's evening time and she's sitting on the edge of the vineyard and talking about a swimming pool she is building behind where she is sat. *'It will be so nice to finish harvest every morning and jump straight in the pool,'* she laughs. A swimming pool seems somewhat necessary for a region where the temperature is known to regularly exceed 40°C (104°F). I dig a little deeper into the nuances of Meli's homeland. Pella, situated in North Greece, in between North Macedonia and the sea, is the former stomping ground of Alexander the Great, as well as the native home of the ancient amphora. It's also the land of ice and fire, with scorching-hot summers and winters that frequently offer a heavy dose of snow. *'When we harvest, we have to be in the vineyards by latest 6am,'* Meli explains. *'Any later and we've lost freshness, both in the grapes and our team!'*

Meli is an oenologist, and daughter of Thomas Ligas – a notorious outsider in the region. The family has always sat at odds with local wine-growers, despite remaining close to Pella's historical and cultural roots. *'My father was known as "Ligas the crazy guy". He started growing grass in the vines and made enemies for it; people thought our vineyards looked untamed. He was determined to work with only our local varieties. Varieties like Roditis, Xinomavro, Kydonitsa, and Limniona. In the 1980s and 90s, other winemakers in Pella were going to France to study oenology and coming back and wanting to replant their family domaines with Merlot and Cabernet Sauvignon because that's what they'd worked with in France.'*

I ask Meli whether it is so black and white, surely there are some indigenous varieties used across Pella? *'Native varieties exist to an extent in the region, but often they are hiding between the international varieties in blends. Besides at one point it was banned to make a single varietal wine with native varieties.'* Roditis, in particular, was a variety in which the Ligas' saw instinctive potential. *'Everyone told us it's a low-acid, low-aroma grape. The best it can do is be blended away. But, my father believed if we planted Roditis in good soils and focused on the root development, we could make complex, mineral wine. We have interesting soils: pink and white granite, limestone, and schist. The soils*

are complex, aided by the erosion of the mountain on which the vineyards are situated. He believed in our terroir so much that he established his own appellation, PGA Pella, in 1993, so he could make the wines he wanted – wines that spoke of the true history of the region. That's him, just always thinking ahead. He built a reservoir in the 1970s. He knew the region would dry out in the future. Now we use this water to give our new vines the start they need – we only irrigate the young vines, as we want them to dig deeper into the soil to find their own identity as they mature, rather than stay drinking water on the surface. This reduces the quantity of fruit, but the quality is much better.'

Clearly Thomas' pioneering vision for Ktima Ligas has provided good grounding for Meli's work. Thomas, now retired, still chips in around the domaine, but Meli is at the helm, and she knows exactly where she wants to go. *'We're fully self-sufficient. We have the reservoir and we were early adopters of solar panels. We're not dependent on anything from outside to run the vineyards and winery.'* Taking over a domaine is no mean feat, especially in the alpha-dominant society of Greece where almost everyone who works at a winery is male. Add that to the fact that Meli and her son Nathan split their time between Pella and Toulouse, and throw in an active wine-import business that she operates across

Wine to try: Roditis Barrique (Ktima Ligas – Pella, Greece)

Northern France – she does seem to be spinning a lot of pipettes. I ask her how she is planning for the future. *'It's my turn to experiment. Five years ago, we planted a vineyard by the forest via a system called "franc de pied". We took cuttings from our own vines and planted them. I want to plant every vineyard like this from now on. It's my vision. The cuttings we plant grow their own roots, rather than needing to be grafted onto American rootstocks as is the norm. This way we can get a better sense of the Pella terroir.'* It's definitely ambitious considering the only guarantor against risks like phylloxera is to use American rootstocks. But Meli is assured. *'The vines that we birth through this system are proving more resistant to disease, shifts in temperatures and the challenges of the local environment. In other news they are truly of the region and adapt themselves to it with ease. Natural wines start with the vine, and this is the closest to their birthplace as they can get.'*

And then there are the grasses, and vegetation she grows in the vineyard to combat the ferocity of the sun. *'Our biggest challenges are drought and heat. Planting grasses, wheat, and wild oats creates moisture at the base of the vine and actually reduces the heat in the soil by 2–4°C (3.6–7.2°F), which makes a significant difference to the vine over the growing season.'* Flowers, beans, and mustard seeds are planted to attract insects like bees, beetles, and worms to boost biodiversity and bring movement and strength to vineyards, particularly to younger vines. Herbs are picked from the local area and stored under the winery to later be made into teas that will be applied to the vine to alleviate certain pressures. Horsetail is gathered and sprayed onto the vines to help combat mildew. Nettles, sourced from the mountain, are rich in minerals and are made into teas to help stimulate the vines, which is particularly useful in tough years, or for younger vineyards needing a boost. Chamomile teas act as an after-sun and are applied after hot periods to help the leaves calm down and recover from any sunburn they have suffered.

It's clear to see the revolutionary spirit runs in the family, and Pella is luckier for it. *'We're seeing our neighbours now starting to appreciate what we've been doing the whole time, and slowly the region is restoring our historical traditions,'* says Meli. I think about the wines, and how despite being so tied to such a specific geographic location, their flavours work so well with so many cuisines. I've paired the wines with Irish, Brazilian, Middle Eastern, Japanese, and Mexican fare, and each wine lifts out a new layer of aroma, flavour, and texture in the dishes they are paired with, with that little bolt of electricity that still catches my breath.

THE TRUTH CATCHER – from nature to bottle

CHRISTINA RASMUSSEN

Obsessive, untiring, and perpetually on the move, wine-grower, writer, and documentarian Christina Rasmussen is a woman with a vision. That vision is to tell the stories of winemakers clearly and truthfully.

A university placement at winery Louis Latour in Beaune caused a 21-year-old Christina to fall in love with the world of wine. *'I knew nothing about wine when I arrived in Burgundy, but it changed the course of my life,'* she once told me over dinner – one of many we've shared in the years since knowing each other. In the years that followed her epiphany, Christina travelled, read extensively, and started to write about wine, both for her own newsletter and for multiple publications whose readers were keen to digest her insatiable appetite for often complex and unusual topics. Natural wine was a key piece of the overall jigsaw puzzle of events that saw Christina truly cement her love for wine and fuel her determination to bring its truth to public awareness. *'It is a very visceral experience to walk in a sensitively and organically farmed vineyard, green and teeming with life, and then see a neighbouring vineyard blasted with herbicide so that the grey earth more closely resembles cement,'* she says.

Christina argues that often, consumers are disconnected from this reality when it comes to choosing which wine to drink.

'This is what appealed to me about natural wine when I first came across the term: it urgently raised dialogue on farming. There was also something both atavistic and soothing in its simplicity; as a millennial who was still relatively new to the world of wine, it was the antipode to the issues of hyper-consumerism and globalization I had grown up with. There was a clear chain from nature to bottle, and it was a reminder that it is still possible to have a connection to the land and nature through the products we consume.'

In 2020, she and her business partners Daniela Pillhofer and Peter Honegger (also co-founders of UK importer Newcomer) birthed Littlewine, a communication platform dedicated to recording the work of natural wine-growers from around the world. In 2023, they changed lanes, transforming Littlewine into the world's first winemaker-led knowledge platform, allowing wine professionals and wine-lovers to subscribe to the platform to access information directly from winemakers, including data on their wines and their vineyards and educational material on wine regions, grape varieties, agriculture, and just about everything else. Christina taught herself to fly a drone and has been around much of the world, documenting the natural winemakers' stories to feed into Littlewine, and having the kind of experiences that reinforce her decision to develop the platform and tell the (often disputed) truth about natural wines. *'A few years ago, when I was in Beaujolais with natural wine-grower Guy Breton (aka P'tit Max), he disappeared to his cellar for a while, returning with a bottle of wine. It was a bottle of Morgon 1989, his second-ever vintage. I was stunned. It's often said that natural wine can't age. Yet, here was this bottle, almost in its third decade, and despite having had no sulphites added, there was tension and energy in that liquid; it was as though the wine was dancing on my tongue. It not only smelt alive, but it also felt alive.'*

This was a wine that had come from one of those green vineyards Christina had experienced during the early stages of her career. *'Tasting the wine, it was clear that the microbial diversity of a healthy vineyard directly impacts not only a wine's flavour but also its evolution. By cultivating*

a healthy soil and environment for your vines, you are also cultivating a healthy microbial population. In turn, these microbes can ferment grapes to create a healthy and unique wine that translates its terroir and is capable of maturing without additions. Sitting in front of me was the man with kind, humble eyes, whose very own hands had farmed that vineyard to cultivate those microbes and make that wine all those years ago. I felt his connection to the land through that glass in my hand. It was deeply personal.'

In the world of wine, there is often a lot of talk of process, particularly in the area of winemaking. Much of the debate about natural wine is built around decisions made in the cellar. Here Christina keeps an open mind to best report the personal, nuanced methods of the winemaker, while focusing on the truly important factor: their agricultural philosophy. *'I sometimes worry that we focus too*

ABV: /2% CONTAINS SULFITES

OWN-ROOTED PALOMINO BUSH VINES PLANTED IN /935, OWNED AND ORGANICALLY FARMED WITH LOVE BY CLINE CELLARS

HAND HARVESTED BY CHRISTINA RASMUSSEN, MEGAN CLINE, ABE SCHOENER & FRIENDS ON /3th AUGUST 20/9

9/10 FOOT-STOMPED, BASKET PRESSED & MOVED VIA TINY BUCKETS TO AN OLD BARREL IN NORTH CHINATOWN, DTLA

/10 DESTEMMED BY HAND AND IMMERSED IN JUICE IN A GLASS DEMIJOHN FOR A MACERATION PERIOD OF EIGHT WEEKS, BEFORE BEING BLENDED INTO THE BARREL

NATURALLY FERMENTED, UNFINED, UNFILTERED. AGED ON THE LEES & BOTTLED IN MARCH 2020 BY ABE & FRIENDS IN THE MIDST OF THE PANDEMIC. 202 BOTTLES PRODUCED

TO ABE & MEGAN — THANK YOU FOR BELIEVING IN ME & SUPPORTING ME.

CHRISTINA RASMUSSEN

Wine to try: The Alley (Christina Rasmussen – Contra Costa County, CA, USA)

much on winemaking details and too little on farming details when it should be the inverse. Some of us may prefer wines made with low intervention, others may prefer wines made with more significant intervention. Many like wines from a large spectrum of winemaking styles. But, together, we should all be united in educating ourselves more about what we can do agriculturally to ensure a brighter future for the land.'

For Christina, the importance lies with transparency – at the core of Littlewine's belief system is that the wine-drinker has a right to know what they are drinking and why it tastes as it does. *'The drinker should be able to know who farmed and made their wine and with which methods and inputs. Only then can they make truly informed decisions. For me, access to these facts is much more important than reading a tasting note or trying to comprehend a score.'*

It's one thing documenting the world of wine-growing and quite another living it. For this reason, Christina jumped at the chance to get her hands dirty, first, in California's Contra Costa County, where she made a single barrel of wine from one of her favourite varieties (old-vine Palomino) in 2019 alongside cherished wine-grower Abe Schoener. Then in 2021, she planted a one-acre 'experimental' vineyard in Oxfordshire, UK, with several varieties propagated via massal selection that she hopes are suited to England's climate.

'I wanted to learn to farm first-hand. Through farming, we can observe, explore, and learn from the endless intricacies that exist in nature. Through farming, we can bring back the truths of soil and plant and translate these into wine.'

The Alley

2019

BRIDGEHEAD VINEYARD PALOMINO, CONTRA COSTA COUNTY, CALIFORNIA, USA

THE NEW GEN REGEN – vinifera under review

SOPHIE
EVANS

Sophie Evans is the UK's vigneron to watch. Farming a modest one-hectare vineyard outside Ashford in Kent, she is teaching herself how to farm truly regeneratively.

I met Sophie on a warm English summer's day in 2019 as we excitedly planted Trousseau vines at Tillingham farm in Sussex. At the time, she was towards the end of a winemaking degree at Plumpton, the UK's leading agricultural college, and was writing a dissertation on essential-oil treatment for vines.

'I had an interest in herbal medicine,' she begins. *'Of course, winemaking degrees don't teach natural science, so I started my own research. I discovered Tim Phillips of Charlie Herring wines in Hampshire. He was the only person I knew of in the UK using essential oils like lavender to slow the development of unwanted fungal issues like botrytis. I've always treated myself with plants, so I figured you must be able to do the same with vines. It all makes sense, really. If you can use these things as an antifungal to clean your wound, or your house, or to relax you before bed, those properties can benefit the vineyard too.'*

Sophie's aim as a wine-grower is to reduce, if not cut out entirely, non-natural sprays. It's a pursuit that has now taken her far and wide in search of a solution. She first travelled to Vermont to work for pioneering wine-grower and botanist Deirdre Heekin of La Garagista. Here on the biodynamically farmed slopes of the most northerly territory in the US, she learned of the power of sowing medicinal herbs between the vines, which could later be turned into natural remedies. It was here Sophie also discovered the potential of hybrid varieties, which taste a little different to vines planted with the usual *Vitis vinifera*, but are much more resistant to many diseases and drastically reduce the number of treatments a vine needs. *'I was always interested in new flavours and odd, rare grape varieties. I like Pinot Noir as much as the next person, but there is a world of flavour out there. While I worked for Deirdre, I fell in love with these new varieties like Frontenac Gris and Brianna,'* Sophie explains.

After harvest wrapped up in Vermont, Sophie headed to Germany where she'd learned of 2Naturkinder in Franconia outside of Frankfurt. There, Melanie Drese and Michael Völker were planting some European hybrids; vines that they considered more disease resistant in a marginal climate. After two harvests, she kept moving, visiting hybrid breeders around Europe.

'I'm convinced [hybrids] are a big part of the future of wine-growing,' says Sophie. *'They can make interesting and complex wines and they are getting better at resisting disease. Some hybrids are also being developed with*

the changing climate in mind, which is crucial as it is becoming harder to grow certain varieties in certain places.'

Sophie was still in Germany when she learned of a tiny plot of vines in a garden in Kent, owned by a young couple who worked in the art industry and were interested in finding someone to tend the vines. *'I was ready to come home,'* she says. *'I missed the UK's wildness … and of course the pubs!'* No doubt she was also ready to put into practice all she had absorbed in her time away.

In 2022, Sophie completed her inaugural vintage of her matchbox-sized vineyard, which is planted with Pinot Gris, Pinot Noir, Bacchus, and Reichensteiner. From it, she crafted three wines, including a blend called Electric Field. *'No doubt I told you about the time I got electrocuted in the field,'* she quips over WhatsApp, sharply piquing my interest.

I ask her how much she is able to live by her 'all-natural' philosophy now she is on her own. Given the UK climate and grizzly summers like 2023, I can't imagine it's a walk in the park. *'I learned from Deirdre to make space to think and not be manic all the time! I'm especially trying to implement a calmer way of doing things, especially during tough years. But I feel very connected to the place now; doing everything myself by hand I've gotten to know the plants*

and the different parts of the vineyard very well. My herbs and flowers are transformed into teas and ferments, and I use some biodynamic practices alongside, which has improved the soil no end. I grow fennel and sage to combat mildew. If you part the plants that grow on the soil surface, you can see the mycelium, and the topsoil is so wonderfully textured.'

This year, Sophie has taken on the farming of another half-hectare nearby, which is planted with an older hybrid called Phoenix, and Schönburger. *'Long term I have a list of hybrids I want to plant,'* she concludes. But for now, she is happy to work on her original mission of growing slowly and listening to what her vineyards needs. *'I feel settled now,'* she concludes. And besides, there's a pub right around the corner.

Wine to try: Electric Field (Sophie Evans – Kent, England)

THE STORYTELLER – the militant mentality
FLEUR GODART

It's 12.30pm Paris time and I'm late again. A perpetual disorder it seems – *'it's genetic'* my friend Tegan shrugs off casually. But this time I can't bear to be five minutes behind, let alone an hour. Not for Fleur Godart and not this weekend. My tardy tornado sweeps into Les Deux Gares, a compact little bistro by the train tracks of Gare de L'Est. Fleur has brought her team to meet me for lunch, and they definitely don't have time for my early morning Eurotunnel dramas. It's the weekend of La Dive Bouteille – the 'Coachella' of natural wine. We are all scheduled up to our eyes over the weekend, starting in just a few hours for Fleur when she will drive down the autoroute A11 and emerge into the Loire to throw a series of tastings, events, and parties over the weekend.

I eye my friend Michael across the table, who has joined for lunch and for one I am glad he is there; he is good at extracting the best stories from people he speaks to, and Fleur's stories I am desperate to hear. I've known Fleur for a few years. As one of the only female distributors I've ever heard of, let alone met, and as founder of Cuvées Militantes – a collaborative wine label that is fast sweeping the UK – I knew I had to catch her here in Paris, and today. Fleur pours me a glass of Alsace Gewürztraminer by a producer called Rietsch. I take a glug, and it tastes like adventures. Fleur turns to me and begins to tell me hers.

Fleur was seventeen and in theatre school. She was there because she wanted to tell stories. Her father was a chicken farmer where they lived in Dordogne.

'We didn't exactly have the best relationship.' Fleur looks at me straight on. *'Everyone always assumes I'm a daddy's girl, but the reality is I stepped in to save his business.'* She was in her first year of theatre school when her father came off his motorbike. He couldn't make it to the market to sell the chickens. He had no way to make a living. *'The chicken industry is like the whole farming industry in France: brutally unsustainable; a toxic system that hasn't worked since the war. The pressure on farmers to scale to industrial levels from the government is catastrophic. There is one suicide every single day in France from within the farming community. It's a disaster. I couldn't risk it with my dad.'* Fleur convinced a fellow student to help her at the market and they turned up with the chickens, ready to give it a go and at least have a laugh.

'There was a winemaker at the market,' Fleur smiles as she digs her hands into the memory. *'Philippe Chaigneau from Château Massereau, Fifi! That bastard! He was so arrogant. He made my blood boil – he still does, even though I love him! It was the first week we were there. I knew nothing about wine, I didn't have any good*

wine around me growing up. I strode over to him and asked for a glass of his best wine. I wanted to take him down a level and tell him his wine wasn't as good as he was telling everyone it was.' She took a swig of the wine. '"Hello" I thought, there's actually someone in here.' She took another. 'Every time I came back to the wine, I got a different impression of it. Jasmine, rose, then spices. Tropical fruits, then coffee. It was like a trip around the world in a glass. I'd joined theatre school because I wanted to tell stories, and now I realized this was the story I wanted to tell. I also realized if I could enjoy this kind of wine without any training, any background, then everyone can.'

I sit back in the booth of the buzzy Parisian bistro listening to the calming clatter of Friday lunch service around me. I wonder if Fleur might have imagined in that moment at the market how the axis of her life would shift and how much she would go on to achieve for the whole of the natural-wine movement. She quit theatre school and went to work for Massereau for a year. 'I did everything,' she remembers. 'I worked in the vineyard, pruning, harvesting, the lot. I worked in the cellar. I learned everything I could. I suppose in a way, it was an opportunity to reset a connection with agriculture, the land, the solitude of the life my dad had endured and a way of understanding a father who had never known how to communicate with me.'

After a year, Fleur moved to Paris. The first plan was to sell Massereau's wine because it wasn't represented in the city. 'So many doors closed in my face. The problem was that the Bordeaux drinkers weren't interested in natural wine and frankly the natural-wine drinkers weren't interested in Bordeaux.' Eventually, Fleur went to work for an import company and made her first female friend in the industry who took her to hunt for new producers for a start-up project in the US. While they were away, Fleur was convinced to start her own distribution business. Again, not the easiest path to walk down as most wine-growers in France sell direct to restaurants and their other customers, but Fleur was determined. 'I told them, "you already have two jobs. You are a grape-grower and a winemaker, why add a third job to your workload by driving all over France to sell your wine, let me do that part for you. It's exactly like your agreements with your foreign importers".' It worked, and Fleur perceived that a sense of legitimacy had been awarded to her through her status as farmer's daughter.

Once she had enough clients, she started selling her father's chickens alongside the wine. I frown, trying to imagine this kind of set up in London. 'Chickens carry terroir, too,' Fleur explains to me unflinchingly. 'Buying chickens from us aligns with restaurants' values, it was an easy sell.'

And so Vins et Volailles was up and away.

And what about Cuvées Militantes? How did that all start? I've got a text-message summary from Fleur sitting in my phone, and the wines have been selling like hotcakes across the wine programs I manage, but I need the full story to make sense of it.

'My whole life I've been harassed, every woman I know has. Once, the chef I worked for pulled out his penis at the end of service and asked me if I could help him with it. This type of shit was honestly normal. Then one night a few years ago my colleague Louise and I were at a magazine launch. The woman who owned the magazine is a brilliant visionary and businesswoman, it was her party. We got into conversation with this middle-aged guy who started making derogatory comments about her, using language that was so out of tone with the kind of woman he was talking about. It was a jolly night, I remember it was summer, we wanted to have a nice time, so we suggested in a light-hearted manner to this guy that he might pull other words from the richness of our language to describe this powerful woman. But instead of taking our point, he blew up. "No one can say anything anymore," he roared. "You're all just* putes féministes (feminist whores)". He stormed out.'

'The next day Louise and I met up for lunch and we couldn't stop talking about it. We were pretty affected by what had happened. We needed to find a way to reclaim the words used against us. We joked about changing the distribution name to Putes Féministes. We were sat there trying to lighten the heaviness of the event when one of our producers Julien Albertus called. He had a dilemma. Julien had 850 extra bottles of skin-contact wine, and he wasn't sure what to do with it. In that moment Cuvées Militantes was born. We bought the lot and labelled it Putes Féministes. We reappropriated the insult and turned it into something meaningful and fun, and most importantly a label on our terms.'

It's a good story, you could say even better than the one that had propelled Fleur into her natural-wine journey in the beginning. Interesting, I thought, for someone who enjoys stories that the stories seem to make their way to her instead.

In the years that have followed, more and more wine-growers have become involved and collaborated in Cuvées Militantes – women and men alike. Now there are thirteen wines under the label. My favourite after Putes Féministes is Sorcières (Witches), a spirited and saline Chardonnay from Athénaïs de Béru in Chablis. As a stand-alone woman in Chablis, particularly in the village of Béru where making your own wine was against popular and political local opinion, Athénaïs was all too familiar with the insult 'witch'. Let's say there was resonance there. But it's not always such an easy win. *'We've had winemakers who have not wanted to get involved because they've had their own problems. Some think it's political enough to be making natural wine, without adding another element to their struggles,'* explains Fleur. *'But often their mentality changes. We had a particular vigneron who didn't want to get involved with us, but later re-approached us saying his daughter was suffering from an eating disorder, and might this have anything to do with patriarchal issues we are trying to address with the Cuvées Militantes? A door opened.'*

'Everyone has a role to play in our world; everyone has responsibilities. We see ourselves as acting in defence of everyone in the wine and hospitality industry. With Cuvées Militantes, we try to plant a seed and see where it goes, see what we can build together. We try and find the right sentiment for the winemaker, something that resonates with them and their own journey or experiences.'

As I kiss Fleur goodbye and wish her *bon chance* for her big weekend, I get the feeling that she is only at the beginning of her stories.

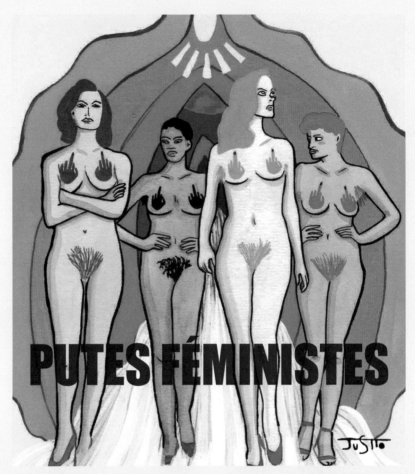

PUTES FÉMINISTES

Wines to try: Putes Féministes (Cuvées Militantes – Alsace, France) and Sorcières (Cuvées Militantes – Burgundy, France)

THE CUSTODIANS – preserving the ancient undergrowth

MONIQUE MILLTON & TIM WEBBER, MANON FARM

I first met Monique Millton and Tim Webber of Manon Farm in 2016. I was in Australia working the harvest, splitting my time between two wineries – Ochota Barrels and Gentle Folk, both in the Basket Range district outside Adelaide. It was a blissful time, having escaped the icy ravages of Danish winter via transplantation to Sydney as part of the noma team. The timing of our arrival couldn't have been any better. After a month of soaking up the Sydney sun by day and pouring wines by night at beloved bistro 10 William Street, I put myself on a plane to Adelaide and spent a very happy month scrabbling around vineyards harvesting grapes, putting together and dismantling basket presses more times than I care to remember, and trying desperately not to mess anything up. It didn't seem to phase me working in two wineries at once. After a decade working in hospitality, in which the hours and conditions might be best described as brutal, I was inured to running between places and lugging awkward-shaped items around.

It turned out that 2016 would prove a pivotal year for the South Australian winemaking community. Many wineries, inspired by restaurant noma's arrival, attempted their first (and last) *sans souffre* (without sulphites) wines. Natural wine, or at least the idea of natural wine, was raging in Sydney, Melbourne, and Adelaide. I have to admit, I adored the wines. Having been raised on Italian DOC and DOCG regulations, winemakers here seemed so free to do things however they pleased, and I found the culture refreshing, and compelling. The wines were equally liberated: juicy and roof-raising, like the kind of person I felt when I drank them. The problem was of course that many of them weren't natural at all. They didn't come from organic or regeneratively farmed grapes. Not many winemakers in South Australia own their own vineyards and as a result many vineyard owners would exercise their prerogative to grow the grapes the way they deemed appropriate. Some, including the wineries I worked for, had great relationships with the growers and were able to sway the farming practices.

Over in the winery the grapes fermented with their natural yeasts, the juice wasn't filtered or fined, but many winemakers ran into problems by choosing to avoid using sulphites, which resulted in maladies in the wine after the tricky vintage that year. In short, the grapes weren't in good enough shape to 'go natural'. By the following year, many winemakers had turned their back on the idea of natural wine and went back to how they'd done things all along.

Of course, in the early months of 2016, I was there in the middle of the story and blissfully unaware, shoulders sunburnt from long mornings picking grapes and trying to dodge alarmingly coloured spiders, legs sticky from weeks of treading, and hands stained an immovable bluey black.

About halfway through my time in the Basket Range, I heard about a couple in the Forest Range who had recently agreed to purchase an old farm with 4.5 hectares of grapes, and who planned to work biodynamically, making wine as close to nature as they could. Monique hailed from New Zealand, and her parents Anne and James Millton helped put biodynamics on the map in the Southern Hemisphere. I drove to see them one morning, craning my neck out the window to catch sight of koalas lazing in the ash trees ahead.

I find Mon and Tim to be an unassuming couple: quiet, pensive, almost otherworldly; encapsulated by the humble but beautiful cabin they are inhabiting while they wait for their new life to begin. Their paths collided in the early years of Rootstock, a minimal intervention wine fair in Sydney, where they both were pouring wines at tables beginning with 'M' – Millton and [Lucy] Margaux. *'It was our destiny,'* smiles Tim. Both passionate farmers, they moved to the Adelaide Hills with the vision of growing produce and living off the land. An opportunity came about to purchase some Pinot

Noir and Pinot Gris from a local grower one year, but it felt all wrong. *'It was like an arranged marriage,'* recalls Mon. *'I grew up growing grapes and these purchased grapes were strangers to us; we hadn't grown them; we didn't know them; we couldn't forge a connection with them.'* The vigneron dream was parked.

During what they refer to as the 'skimp months', they would forage for mushrooms and once came upon an old property with vineyards that had been up for sale for years. *'We didn't have two guineas to rub together, but the the bank was crazy enough to support two young agriculturalists, so we secured a loan and were able to put together a small offer, far below what the owners had originally wanted for it.'*

I ask them why no one else wanted the property, perhaps a winery. *'The vineyards are small and poky, some steep and rocky, it was worthless to a commercial winery wanting to achieve anything on a real commercial scale. And there were so many different varieties,'* laughs Mon, *'we inherited Pinot Noir, Pinot Gris, Chardonnay, Sauvignon Blanc, Merlot, Cabernet Sauvignon, Cabernet Franc, and Italian variety Garganega. Oh, and then there was Savagnin!'*

I tilt my head wondering how the previous owners had the foresight to plant Europe's current heartthrob

MONIQUE MILLTON & TIM WEBBER

variety a quarter of a century ago. *'They thought it was Albariño, it turns out it was Savagnin, and it was all over South Australia by the time anyone realized! Anyway, we planted more of that and some more Italian varieties like Aleatico and Malvasia which are well suited to our climate.'*

The hardest part of the journey was the road that lay ahead after they took over the vineyards, officially establishing Manon Farm. *'The first few years were tough. The vines had been farmed conventionally until we moved in. We were young and completely idealistic. We stopped all the sprays and instead invested our time in making teas and herbal tinctures. We pulled out the irrigation. We wanted the vines to find their own strength.'*

Mon remembered attending a talk by biodynamic visionary Nicolas Joly. *'He said when you start to convert the vines, it's like dealing with junkies. And he was completely right, our vines were junkies, and we'd removed their vices. The natural yeasts weren't strong enough and we struggled at the beginning.'*

I ask about the climate and if they have noticed any shifts associated with climate chaos. *'The hills have a moderate climate. The summers are warm and dry, and the winters are cool and wet. But after 2019, there was no more rain.'* Mon and Tim continued

to their holistic work on their vines, using the plants around them, such as chamomile, to cool the vines.

In mid-2019 Australia burst ablaze and megafires, caused by lack of moisture in the soil, scorched the country, reducing twenty-four-million hectares to ash. *'It was a dark, scary time. I thought why on earth are we planting these vines, these European plants, when our whole country is on fire? The fires burned around us, but luckily Manon was spared. A group of forty kangaroos moved into the vineyards, and we offered up our farm to them. We let them eat the grapes that year (what was left was forged into a blend simply called Table Red).'* Mon and Tim now carry out 'controlled fires', around the farm on a yearly basis – an ancient practice designed to renew the topsoil and avoid these kinds of disasters. The knowledge, which for a century was shamefully suppressed, is re-emerging now.

Over a recent FaceTime catch up I ask them what natural wine means to them and how they go about their truly 'hands off' approach. *'Actually, that part is pretty straightforward,'* Mon grins at me through the screen. *'Because we work with the biodynamic calendar, we only work in the cellar during descending moon phases, the gentlest and most grounded time to move the wine and plan our cellar work. We're only in the cellar for about three days a month, the rest of the time we are in the vines and the rest of the farm.'*

They also use the calendar to know when the preparations are ready to apply, or when to expect certain weather patterns, which are connected to planetary rhythms and partly predictable. Central elements of biodynamics play a big part at Manon, but only the elements that make sense in the context of the land on which they work. They don't have cows or sheep, or any hard-footed animals as mentioned in Steiner's work. *'Our soil is fragile and holds an ancient seedbank, we don't want to have them in the vineyard and create compaction. Instead, we have kangaroos that are soft-footed and tread the ground carefully.'* They use cow manure from the farm next door and their friend and fellow winemaker Julien Castagna gifted them cow horns for their biodynamic preparations. They apply preparation #501 (a mixture of quartz silica designed to stimulate photosynthesis and develop the aroma of the grapes) only once a year, as the vineyards already have high levels of quartz. They don't need much help in that department. They also mix their veggie and fruit leftovers with the manure to make compost, which rapidly increases microbes in the soil. Herbs and flowers such as calendula, yarrow, sage and lavender are planted in the hedgerows alongside the vines and are crafted into sprays for the vine canopy. Each plant plays its own role in keeping the vines healthy and free from disease, and dramatically reduces the need to spray copper and sulphur in the vineyards. There are also elements Manon use that don't grow on the farm. Seaweed is brought from the ocean and made into a tea to dry out the vines during humid periods and protect against mildew.

'The idea is to create life. To keep the life multiplying, alive, happy, and humming. Chemicals can do the opposite – they suppress, kill off, and make environments out of balance, creating disharmony and disease. Biodynamics is the pursuit of life and philosophy. It seeks to answer questions like how are we here? We humans are not in charge; we are part of planetary systems but for a long time we removed ourselves from theory or thought. Philosophies like biodynamics are seen as alternative but they really aren't. They are everyday life for all living things. If you look at the Geoponika texts, they cover so much ancient wisdom that has been around for thousands of years. Ultimately, we are not making wine, we are making medicine. And we are not winemakers; we are custodians of our land, and when you taste our wines, they are youthful, which is funny because our land is so ancient.'

Wine to try: Geoponika (Manon Farm – Forest Range, Australia)

THE (BENEVOLENT) BRUTE – building Barcelona's Brutal

STEFANO
COLOMBO

In November of 2013 a small wine bar on Barcelona's Carrer de la Princesa exploded into life. Imagined by Venice-born industrial-designer-cum-hospitalitarian Stefano Colombo, Catalan winemaker Joan Ramon Escoda, importer Joan Valencia (of Cuvée 3000), and Stefano's chef brother Max, Bar Brutal rapidly became a cultural flagship for natural wine in Europe, evoking a very visceral sense of *carpe diem* from within its patrons.

'It's our fault; it's in the name,' concedes Stefano, *'we named the bar Brutal, and it was kind of catchy; people come to have their brutal experience. We've had some very, very late nights in that bar.'*

I've known Stefano since 2015, after meeting in Copenhagen, and it's easy to see how someone with such vivacity and infectiousness of character could have established a bar with such a relentless global following. I ask him what inspired him in the first place. *'Everything starts with passion, about natural wine and the people involved,'* he begins. *'I visited Copenhagen for the first time in 2011 where I met Sune from Rosforth & Rosforth and ate at noma. Everywhere I turned, people were popping these insane bottles, and I thought to myself, "Who is drinking all these bottles?" I knew that if they could create this culture here, then we could do it back in Barcelona where* we were only a few hours from all this natural wine production. I told myself, "No more excuses".'

'We opened, and the first five years were pretty intense. Within the first six to eight months, we were broke. It's not that people weren't coming – it's more that they didn't want to pay the prices for the wines. You have to remember that back then, a glass of conventional wine in a wine bar in Barcelona cost between one to two euros, while at Brutal, we were selling these weird orange wines at five to six euros. People were rejecting bottles and glasses. It started to get complicated, and we were running out of cash.'

'But at the foundation of every great place, it's about the people. We had a really strong and committed staff at that time; Nuria Remon (now a full-time winemaker under the same name) was our sommelier. We came together and asked ourselves what we could do. We'd built up this cellar full of wine, it was our only asset. We said, "If we're going to die, we're not going to die sober!" I told the team, "If I can't pay you, I'll pay you with the bottles from the cellar." These crazy guys would open their bottles, their "salaries", mid-service to drink them and share them with guests. They said, "I don't care; this is my bottle, my salary, I want to share it with people." That culture sparked a sort of euphoria and excitement, and people started to come to see what was going on.'

'That's how we started this movement: for the love of wine; the love of people. Now everyone is paid well, and we have over two-thousand natural wines in the cellar. We expanded the space to fit another thirty covers: we're open seven nights a week. It's gotten out of hand! Everyone wants to come, drink, and buy a t-shirt. Sometimes I think we sell more t-shirts than wine!'

Bar Brutal turns ten this year. I ask Stefano if much has changed over ten years in the way he and his restaurant approach things.

'The restaurant has definitely grown up, and so have we. After Covid we put a lot of our efforts into staff training. It's hard to find good people these days, so when we find someone we like we really invest in their knowledge. Covid forced us to evolve due to social distancing, which meant we had to step up the food offering, but the team were ready for it. They were growing up, too. We store the wines under proper temperature control, and we keep them in the cellar for longer; we drink less. Five years ago, we would open bottle after bottle after bottle because we wanted to taste every new vintage that came in. It was all about everything all at once. We have so much respect for the craftsmanship and passions of the vignerons. Now we open fewer bottles but take time to think more about what the wine is saying to us and how it is evolving.'

Catalunya is still the beating heart of natural wine in Spain, but the rest of the country and its islands are fast catching up, making it one of the largest and most dynamic natural wine-producing countries in the world. 'In Catalunya every month there's a new organic grower, and we can claim to have had a part in that. We paved a lot of the way for the new generations to change the way their parents did things. We gave them a platform to tell their stories.'

'Outside of Catalunya, people are trying to make organic wine in 'old-world' Spanish territories: new Rioja, new Ribeira, new Galicia. These wines are more complex than just Glou-Glou style. There's a reason that people love these old-school, very beautiful styles of wine. The connection between the old-school and the new-school is that both sides are trying their best to make a wine that is memorable. At the beginning, natural wine was political – it was anti-establishment – of course, it still is, but now it's more normalized. There are as many natural-wine festivals as music festivals! I'm happy for new generations to have choices and new ways of drinking wine. At the end of the day, when people are connected to wine, they can't not have a good experience; it's an energetic connection to the earth. It's a gift.'

Wine to try: Els Bassots (Escoda-Sanahuja – Catalunya, Spain)

THE CELLAR MASTER – a natural inventory

AVA MEES
LIST

Ava Mees List is deep in thought as I walk into Copenhagen's Hart Bakery to meet her. As restaurant noma's Head Sommelier, she has recently returned to the city after a three-month-long pop-up at the Ace Hotel, Kyoto, during which time the entire team transferred over to Japan. There, they successfully planned, opened, operated, and then closed a restaurant before heading back to re-open the landmark site back in Copenhagen. *'During my whole time in Japan,'* she relects, *'I had maybe one wine that wasn't totally perfect. Natural wine is kept and served so meticulously; it's inspirational.'*

Japan is, of course, well known for its painstaking approach to detail and process. As one of the most powerful markets for natural wine in the world, and an early adopter of the movement, it makes sense that the storage of natural wine there is handled scrupulously. I think of certain wine bars I've worked in around the world, and the sometimes-sorrowful storage of bottles in rooms well above room temperature – upright and balancing bravely on their bases. These venues often have little choice, particularly those situated in the same capital cities that have been so eager to nudge natural wine into the broader cultural conscience in the first place. Wine storage is a perennial problem for sommeliers and operators whose every potential inch turns into a perilous game of Tetris. But, there is one thing these venues all have in common, a sort of supposed saving grace – these wines aren't meant to hang about for long. By their rumoured nature, natural wines are thought to be best in their youth – made young, shipped young, stored young, and ultimately drunk 'fresh off the boat'. Of course, I know this to be untrue. As someone who has bought, sold, and served natural wine for a decade, I've tried some spectacular zero zero wines over the years – many ten to twenty years old and beyond – which displayed jaw-dropping vigour and assuredness. And this is my motive for luring Mees to meet me on a pensive summer's morning in the Danish capital. She is my key to understanding the intellectual architecture behind noma's cellaring program and how natural wines actually thrive and improve given patience and the right amount of time.

Born in New York to a Dutch mother and an American father who worked in theatre, Mees arrived at hospitality via an anthropology degree that she dryly writes off as 'the world's most expensive bartender training', followed by a brief stint in the vintage retail sector. Not exactly what you might envisage as prerequisites for leading the world's most formidable natural-wine program, but Mees is adamant that her early experience continues to serve her.

'I ran a shop in Amsterdam, and I was the only person on the floor. The owner empowered me to stand up for myself. If anyone ever asked to see the manager, I would say, "Hi, that's me". You can imagine that kind of mentality comes in useful from time to time.'

In 2015, Mees moved to Paris and took a position at Saturne, a restaurant that was known to possess the largest library of natural wines in Europe. 'In a cellar that is so expansive, with so many cuvées and vintages, you need to keep things dynamic and work through them. I learned this at Saturne. Working with that kind of list, the trick is to keep the balance. If we had just a few bottles of one wine or vintage left, I'd need to guide the guests to try something else to keep the library alive and stop wines from selling out.'

January 2019 saw Mees migrate to Copenhagen, where she began to work at noma under former Head Sommelier Mads Kleppe, taking over the reins in 2022. Noma's cellar works differently from that of Saturne: 'Not everything is presented to the guest. The wine list is a curation from the wider collection, allowing us to select what is tasting best, the vintages that are showing their full potential. We could easily have multiple wines from the same producer, but we have the privilege of being able to decide on behalf of the guest and reduce any confusion, particularly when you consider we have 3,000 references.' A cellar of 3,000 cuvées is a somewhat jaw-dropping amount of wine, and must be, by anyone's judgement, financed by a serious and sustained belief that it's a good idea. 'Time is patience and patience is money. Noma has always seen wine as an investment. A cellar of its size isn't something that appears overnight; it grows over time – in the case of noma, twenty years.'

I ask Mees gingerly what it takes (apart from money and time) to build that kind of library, knowing full well there's more to it. I know noma would never purchase anything made at any real commercial scale, so they're likely dealing with a plethora of growers from every corner of the globe. 'You need to prove yourself to growers and importers by building long-standing relationships over years and doing things like paying your bills on time. And then, of course, if you sell a lot of wine, you need to buy a lot of wine.' I cast my mind to the noma wine-pairing option and the amount of each wine Mees must need to secure to last the length of any given dish. 'That's actually pretty straightforward. If you know that you want a certain wine by a certain grower, ordering in large quantities awards you a lot of buying power, particularly if there's a relationship there. I suppose the status of a restaurant might also help,' Mees winks.

So, what happens when the wine arrives, I ask. Does Mees list some of it straight away like other venues inevitably would? *'No, most wine is rested for at least a year, sometimes two, and often much longer. We want to let the bottles calm down after their travels to let any potential flaws even out,'* Mees explains.

I think back to every unsettled wine I've ever served and muse wistfully over the prospect of an extended chill time for the precious allocations I have to fight for, pay upfront for, rearrange my matchbox-sized fridges for. Wines that are quite clearly incensed from all the upheaval. Mees is already reading my mind. *'The funny thing is that people think these wines need to be drunk young, but, more often than not, they are drunk too young. Then there's the fact that natural wines are becoming more popular; demand is on the verge of outweighing supply, which means these wines are being consumed before we can see what they would become. During Covid, we caught a bit of a break, and demand slowed down. It felt like the wines were able to just take a minute and relax. Although some take too long; we've waited thirteen years and counting for one cuvée to sort itself out,'* she confesses, *'but it hasn't happened yet! In any case, I don't specifically believe all wines need a decade before they are drinkable – young, fresh wines are sometimes delicious!'*

I turn to the topic of what happens to those bottles over time in noma's cellar. Does Mees think natural wines age in the same way as their conventional counterparts? *'If you work with more industrially made wines, you have a different perspective of keeping a cellar. It's easier, more linear. You can revisit a wine in six months or five years and observe a clear line of evolution. With conventional wines, the focus is on breaking down the tannins or oak flavours, and, again, the evolution of a natural wine isn't as straight lined. Natural wines are alive, and you have to approach them as such. Through a larger range of acidity, they can evolve in several directions, while keeping tension and brightening up the fruit in the bottle. If no sulphites have been added during the winemaking process, a little carbon dioxide can help protect a wine, and keep it fresh, almost locked in time. Live material in the wine continues to keep the wine going if kept in the right conditions. Skin contact on white wines protects against oxidation. Even Glou-Glou wines that we drink in the sunshine for their lightness, freshness, drinkability, can become different wines altogether after a little ageing. They retain the fruit, but other characters start to show up. Some varieties evolve in a discernible direction. Trousseau, for example, starts life with a raw, animalistic quality, which after six, seven, or eight years in the cellar transforms to reveal this amazing* purity of fruit. A few times over the last few years, I have been given Trousseau in a blind tasting and thought it was Poulsard or Pinot Noir, and it turns out to be Trousseau that's been cellared.' In other words, it has come of age.

There is clearly a lot of nuance involved, and a considerable amount of experience working with natural wines is required to know when a wine will be in its prime. 'Knowing when it's the best time to serve a natural wine comes down to the experience of being a natural-wine sommelier. The challenge is to establish when a wine is ready or if the wine is in its last moments.'

As a long-term eyewitness of natural wine's physical evolution, I wonder what Mees makes of the evolution of its perception. 'Interest has exploded; it just grows and grows! It's in all these memes now! There has definitely been a change in the character of wine-drinkers. Young people are investing in all these culinary excursions. Wine-lovers are no longer confined to suits, they wear jeans and sneakers, and that is thanks to natural wine. People are using their wine passion as an expression of self; for them, it's all about cultural knowledge.'

On the other hand, as a senior manager of the former World's Best Restaurant, Mees has had her fair share of those who say they simply don't like the taste. 'I find it strange when people say they don't like organic wine. They'd never say that about their steak. People will eat the strangest things, but their imagination for some reason can't stretch to wine.'

'Even at a basic level, we accept complexity in things like cheeses and meats, but there are still so many people who think wine should be simplified or familiar. Our strongest wine on the pairing menu at the moment is a cloudy Slovakian wine called Nigori – a reference to the coarsely filtered style of sake of the same name. We call it our "troublemaker". We tell any worried-looking guests, "Just hold off and try it with the food!"'

It comes as no surprise that the restaurant that captured the zeitgeist of an era has supported natural wine for so many years. I ask Mees if anyone at the top ever questions her choices. 'I have free reign over what I decide to buy, serve, and cellar. Well, until someone says "basta!"' she laughs. 'Even with the pairing, which is ordered by seventy per cent of noma's guests, René Redzepi, chef and creator/co-owner of noma and the team instil absolute trust in my work. At the Japan pop-up, staff at the hotel would ask me, "Who signs off the pairing?" and I would just look at them and say, "Me – Hi, that's me".'

Wine to try: Nigori (Strekov 1075 – Slovakia)

THE GO-GIRL – fermenting for freedom

KETEVAN
BERISHVILI, GOGO

I still remember tasting Ketevan Berishvili's Saperavi wine in the Rosforth & Rosforth offices (see page 139) in the summer of 2016. Rosforth & Rosforth already imported a myriad of Georgian wines – too many I remember thinking on several occasions when trying to figure out how on earth to sell them.

Back then, I loved the idea of Georgian wines. Made in a country that is arguably the global birthplace of wine from an assortment of entirely indigenous varieties not found anywhere else on earth. Crafted (more often than not) by small-scale artisans, working without chemicals and almost entirely by hand. Yes, the Georgian dream was very much alive in me in 2016, especially when drinking the wines via the Georgian drinking horn we kept at work. But then came Keti's GoGo wines, and it felt like the last piece of the puzzle fell into place. Every sip felt light-footed yet powerful, layered yet shockingly refreshing. I didn't only love how the wines made me feel, I was hooked on the taste. Now on her eighth vintage, Keti – as she is known in the wine-growing community – has truly cemented herself as one of Georgia's most adept young winemakers, creating singular wines with detail and dexterity.

Daughter to musicians from Georgia's capital Tbilisi, Keti would lend her father a hand, when he moved out of the city – to Artana, the region where wine was first discovered some 8,000 years ago. After years of working in a bank and spurred on by her friends, Keti became a full-time wine-grower and maker, committing to making natural wines under the GoGo label.

'2015 was the first year I decided to try and make wine my way. With a big push from my friends! I named the winery GoGo because it has different meanings. Firstly, it means "girl" and "daughter" – I am a very proud daughter of my father. It also means something like "drive", or "energy". And it's an easy name, simplicity is something I like.'

Now Keti shares a cellar with her father which is nestled in the foothills of the Tsiv-Gombori mountains and the Alazani River, an area known for its awe-inspiring natural beauty, and its key indigenous grape varieties. Keti owns seven and a half acres of vineyards, which lie between three rivers, and grows only native varieties such as Mtsvane, Rkatsiteli, and Saperavi, which she farms and processes as naturally as possible.

'Georgian wine doesn't necessarily mean natural, but, maybe because of our history and traditional way of winemaking, people think that all wine made here is natural,' she corrects me

as I gush romantically over the idea of her homeland. *'We use traditional qvevri as a vessel to ferment and age our wines, but again, this isn't strictly tied to a universally natural approach. Our country is quite small and wine was something that we kept until now as a deep-rooted tradition. Even after the Soviet times, when people left the countryside and moved to Tbilisi the capital, they were still making wine in their garages. My grandfather was a musician who moved to Tbilisi but that didn't stop him from planting a vineyard right in the city centre!'*

It's clear to see that wine runs deep in the blood of Georgians. With its 8,000-year history, I feel almost shy asking Keti what she has learned so far in her first eight since setting up GoGo.

'Actually, a lot has changed and every year we reflect on what has happened, even on our own faults! The biggest change for me was really falling in love with my vineyard. When I decided to make wine, I wasn't thinking about the vineyard. It seemed more interesting to be in the cellar, making wine. But then I realized the vineyard is truly where I want to be.'

'And of course, there is the one thing that never changes,' she adds, *'the worry about the upcoming year. Will the vines be ok? How will the wine turn out?'*

The relentless thrum of trepidation over future harvests is one that every winemaker must learn to live with, especially those who choose not to work with chemicals, and therefore have no access to tweaks or quick fixes should a vine in the vineyard or a wine in the cellar take a turn. And yet, there is something extraordinary that drives these artisans, year after year.

'I want to spread the energy that is in the bottles I make, this is what is most important to me. When you drink wine, you should find joy! Of course, every year is different, never the same, but often the energy in the wines is alike. I often change the labels to reflect a year – to represent something unique, such as feelings, emotions, and stories of my life as a person, and as a winemaker.'

'I think for Georgian people, we make wine to preserve our freedom, but then again after drinking wine we have a different understanding of the term "freedom"!'

Wine to try: Tiamora Rkatsiteli (GoGo Wine – Kakheti, Georgia)

THE MOUNTAINEER – the return to tradition

EDDIE CHAMI, MERSEL WINE

Eddie Chami is a man with pretty serious plans: revive Lebanon's indigenous varieties and work on the country's wine identity. *'For so long it was just copy-paste French varieties, French winemaking techniques. Lebanon has these ancient varieties, no one knows about them. I'm trying to change that.'*

Australian-born to first generation Lebanese migrants, Eddie grew up making arak – a middle-eastern spirit made from distilled wine and anise – at home with his family in Sydney. *'I had to make wine to make arak,'* Eddie shares, *'and then mastering the art of winemaking became a piece of the puzzle I needed to complete.'* Feeling the pull back to his ancestral roots of Lebanon, Eddie moved from Sydney to winemaking school at UC Davis, California, and then on to the Beqaa Valley, Lebanon, where he worked for seven years at a local winery making 'copy-paste' wines: 'tannic reds, and oaky whites' that, though sold well, Eddie sensed didn't tell of the story of Lebanon's history or ancient terroir the way they should.

'I was working at this winery in 2013 making natural wines on the side for me and my friends – skin contacts, and pét-nats. In Lebanon there was no commercial demand for these kinds of wines, but we loved them and we drank them ourselves.' For a while that was all there was to it. At the same time, a worrying pattern was starting

to emerge in the Beqaa Valley: the country's sweetheart wine-growing region was quickly warming. *'Every year we would increase by 2°C (3.6°F), and harvest two days earlier.'*

Towards the end of Eddie's time in the Beqaa Valley, harvests had shot forward from mid-August to the end of July. *'It's hard to keep making good wine when the temperature keeps creeping up, the heat is too much and many of the wines have started to taste thick and soupy.'* In more ways than one it was time to seek higher ground.

In 2019, Eddie and his wife Michelle set up Mersel Wine and started planting vines in the Maksar Mersel region, only a ninety-minute drive away from Beqaa but far up in the mountains where the altitude varies between 1,800–2,500 metres (5,905–8,202 feet) above sea level, making it the highest viticultural area in Europe/Middle East. *'It's only recently that grapes have ripened properly up here,'* Eddie adds. *'Until not long ago the land was snow-capped all year round. But we are lucky, the region is still cool and the mountain air is clean and dry.'* This means the vineyards don't need to be sprayed with pesticides or herbicides and are as a result completely organic. Primordial indigenous varieties such as Merwah, Dhaw al-Qamr, Mariameh, and Marini thrive here and are particularly resistant to

LEBNANI ABYAD *by* MERSEL WINE

Wine to try: Lebnani Abyad (Mersel Wine – Maksar Mersel, Lebanon)

the usual vine plights, like types of mildew, especially if they are grafted onto their own rootstocks and not American rootstocks, which is today the global norm.

It certainly checks out that the varieties that flourish are those that have been here all along, telling the story of one of the world's first winemaking sites. There are some international varieties around – Eddie planted Sauvignon Blanc, Cinsault, and Sangiovese because they are varieties he had worked with before in Australia. *'But they have no real place here, except for Cinsault in the mid altitudes of the valley and Sauvignon Blanc in the higher elevations,'* Eddie admits, *'eventually I will replace them.'*

When it comes to winemaking, there is only one way, the traditional way. *'If my great-grandfather had made wine, he wouldn't have had a cellar full of steel tanks, that's for sure. We honour Lebanese traditions by using local amphora and making wine naturally, which means no filtering or fining, and very little if any sulphites.'*

The only pinch point is trying to ensure all the wines have fermented by the time the snow starts to fall at the start of December, but Eddie relishes the nuances created in the wines either way.

I ask Eddie why making natural wine is so important to him beyond being a good future ancestor for future Lebanese generations. He muses...

'My experience making unnatural wines put me off enjoying them; very few consumers are aware what goes into conventional wine, I think they would drink differently if they did. The international wine-drinking community appreciate our natural wines made with indigenous varieties, and we are embedding our history and culture in our wines. We are a warm, hospitable and unique people, and we want to transfer our soul into our wine for the world to enjoy.'

THE DISRUPTOR – from radical to RAW

ISABELLE LEGERON

If one person can truly claim to have single-handedly created a sea change in the world of natural wine, it's Isabelle Legeron. Not exactly a road for the faint of heart, Isabelle became France's first female Master of Wine in 2009, before giving herself the name 'That Crazy French Woman' and turning her hand to revolutionizing what we imbibe. First, there were her RAW WINE fairs started in 2012 in London (they now take place annually in Paris, Copenhagen, Montreal, Toronto, LA, New York City, and Berlin), swiftly followed by her first book in 2014, *Natural Wine: an introduction to organic and biodynamic wines made naturally* (CICO Books), which provided a detailed and compassionate introduction to natural wines and the artisans behind the movement.

I have met Isabelle a handful of times, our first introduction being a doting email I sent her in 2011 after reading some of her work. I devoured her book when it was published and was a regular visitor to her fairs in London and Berlin. A happy coincidence led to us both attending the inaugural biodynamic course 'Root Time' hosted by wine-grower Gut Oggau in Austria's Burgenland. Over the wet spring of 2023 I got to know much of her journey while we performed tasks like mixing cow manure and water with our bare hands – to make biodynamic preparations, of course…

'I was born in Cognac, my family have made Cognac for generations. I was brought up working in the vineyard, which I naturally hated! I wasn't interested in wine at all. It was what you could call a paysan upbringing; we only ate what we grew or raised, and I was taught to be very resourceful. If you gave me a whole pig, I would probably still know what to do with all of it!' she laughs. *'My family were practical people; they worked hard in the vines and fields – in Cognac you have to grow a lot to make ends meet. In the 1970s, they stopped using manure from my grandmother's cows as fertilizer and started using chemical fertilizer to boost our production levels. Back then no one knew that they were polluting the earth or that what they were doing was wrong. Chemical fertilizer is incredibly strong, so then came the weed killers and then the fungicides onto our land. We started using machines to harvest rather than doing it by hand. I'm incredibly grateful for so much of what my family instilled in me growing up, but their new approach to farming didn't feel right, and I didn't want to be a part of it. I left France and moved to London.'*

It was only later at the age of twenty-eight, after the sudden death of her father, that Isabelle experienced what she calls her 'Saturn Return' and felt the pull back to wine. *'I decided to follow the traditional path. I studied my way up through the Wine & Spirit Education Trust until I ended* up on the Master of Wine course. It's funny because my main motivation was to make some friends in the industry and have a sense of community. If I'd known what the MW truly entailed, I don't think I would have done it!' And yet four years later Isabelle became the first French woman to carry the globally revered title, picking up accolades along the way such as the Madame Bollinger award for Excellence in Tasting and the Villa Maria Award for Viticulture. 'It was all quite corporate and stiff, but I did well,' she remembers. 'I was visiting a lot of very commercial vineyards, but then I started visiting smaller artisan wine-growers who had these incredible philosophies about farming and winemaking. Vignerons like Nicolas Joly, who were working biodynamically – were artisans who really got their hands dirty. Everything really started to change for me.'

When the RAW WINE fair started in 2012, it was clear that Isabelle had begun to create for herself the community she had sought in the early days of returning to wine. In the cities in which they were organized, hundreds of like-minded wine-growers were able to connect not only with wine-lovers but also their fellow growers from around the world, sharing know-how and encouraging each other. 'What RAW WINE offers is visibility and connection for everyone involved. We help unrepresented wine-growers find the right importers for them in that market and introduce drinkers to their new favourite wines.'

Occasionally criticized for her relaxation of maximum sulphite levels in the wines allowed at the fairs, Isabelle is reflective yet unyielding. 'I used to be a lot more hardline when I was younger about things like adding sulphites in winemaking – I would get upset, and I became sick. That approach was not helping anyone. RAW WINE is about farming, first and foremost. Organic or biodynamic agriculture and minimal-intervention winemaking. People are at different stages of their journey: not everyone is in the headspace to make zero zero wines, but twenty-five to thirty per cent of the wine-growers that come to the fair don't add any sulphites at all, and the vast majority add only a tiny amount – we have reduced the maximum levels of sulphites allowed in bottles at RAW WINE from seventy parts per million to fifty to channel this. Most importantly, the wine has to be alive and be a representation of that place at that moment. Natural and low-intervention wine only accounts for one per cent of the wine made around the world. My mission is to grow the market so these incredible wine-growers can sell their wines and get the visibility they deserve. I'm committed to my work because I love nature, and that's what drives everything we do. Natural wine is a way of being. It's an awareness of nature – I think you either have it or you don't.'

The artisan wine fair

—

23-24 April 2023

RAW WINE®

Explore the exciting world of low-intervention organic, biodynamic and natural wines, alongside other craft drinks.

Taste hundreds of wines and meet the growers and makers who created them.

Book tickets at
rawwine.com

—

#rawwineLA
#rawwineweek
@rawwineworld

RAW WINE®
Los Angeles 2023

City Market Social House
1145 South San Pedro Street
Los Angeles CA 90015

Open to the trade & public

Sunday 23rd April
11am - 6pm

Monday 24th April
10am–5pm

Grown naturally, made naturally

Wine fair: Poster for RAW WINE 2023 (Los Angeles, USA)

Wine to try: Les Belemnites (Peggy et Jean-Pascal – Jura, France)

THE LADY OF THE SUNSHINE – the 'slo' grow

GINA GIUGNI, CHENE VINEYARD

It's mid-afternoon as we pull down onto California's Highway 101, the road that connects central California to its coast and that will lead us to the vineyards and winery of biodynamic wine-grower Gina Giugni.

With harvest just around the corner, it's a particularly beautiful time to be in California, with grapes suspended from their vines, the landscape awash with dense colour and a soft, humming warmth. Despite the heat in the air, it's been a cooler year than the region has experienced in the previous handful of vintages, and the general feeling is a positive one: a little prolonged hang-time for the grapes before harvest will only add to the complexity of Californian wines made this year. And besides, a little extra time for surfing and camping trips before the harvest hustle begins can only be considered a bonus. But there is a worry that pricks the air; disease pressure is mounting, particularly in areas like the Edna Valley and the newly established San Luis Obispo (SLO) coast AVA where Gina and her husband Mikey farm their vineyards. With the prolonged wait until harvest, wine-growers are on high alert.

'Gina's going to meet us in the vineyard,' Mikey explains as we enter the winery. He's picked up pizza on the way, and after we leave later that evening, they will work into the night, clearing each vine's airways.

This will be achieved by removing excess leaves and debris so the vines can benefit from airflow and the cooling Pacific winds – in an attempt to ward off the fungal disease that threatens to sabotage a year's work. Farming is seldom easy, particularly without the everyday arsenal of chemicals that come readily available to conventional growers, but it's fair to say Gina's path in life has equipped her better than most to deal with its challenges. From a young age, she was initiated into the world of regenerative farming after her parents bought an eighty-six-acre farm in the Sierra Foothills. In 2001, fourteen acres were dedicated to vines; Rhône varieties that were well suited to the warm, dry climes of Northern California. In 2008, the farm was certified biodynamic by Demeter, which is particularly impressive for a farm of its size. *'Summers were always spent in the vineyard helping my dad,'* Gina remembers. *'Sometimes unwillingly, but I'm thankful now. I always helped with the fermentations in the winery; that was always willingly, I loved it.'*

During college, Gina worked in a tasting room in Sonoma. *'It was the first time I fell in love with Pinot Noir, a variety that was novel to me as my family didn't grow or make it. It was definitely the stepping stone into discovering wine on my own terms, something that was very important to me, coming from a winemaking*

Wine to try: Chene Vineyard Chardonnay (Lady of the Sunshine – CA, USA)

family. I transferred colleges and changed majors from biology to winemaking. I chased Pinot down to the Central Coast of California to SLO, where I got my oenology degree, and worked my first harvest in the cellar for a Pinot Noir producer in Edna Valley, just a stone's throw from where I farm one of the vineyards.'

From there, Gina left California in search of more work experience, which took her to biodynamic wineries in New Zealand's Central Otago, France's Beaujolais, and back to the US, in Oregon and Napa. *'Many places I worked at were farming with biodynamics in the vineyard, but then in the winery, they were defaulting to conventional ways of making wine. It was baffling to see the vineyard farmed with such intent but then the wines to be made just as a recipe. I wanted to farm with biodynamics and make wine with natural chemistry, native yeast, old oak barrels, etc., staying as true to the vineyard terroirs as possible.'*

In 2017, Lady of the Sunshine was born. *'It was so small! Just a few barrels!'* she reminisces. The following year Gina discovered a six-and-a-half-acre vineyard called Chene on the slopes of the Edna Valley, cementing her future as both farmer and winemaker. *'It was a natural transition, which felt very unnatural at the time as I was learning everything as I was going. My dad was my mentor via phone calls, and my husband, Mikey, taught me to drive the tractor. It was full of learning curves, stress, and happy and sad tears, but a very beautiful transition. It wasn't until I started farming that I felt like I truly connected to the real joy of making wine. Spending every single day in the vineyard, tending to the vines, the soil, the weeds, the pests, experiencing the rain and sunshine and wind and heat – I felt I truly understood how wine can speak of place. It helped bring the idea of terroir full circle for me. Being a true vigneron, immersed in every stage within the cycle, has been what I have fallen in love with. I can't have one without the other now. Farming and making wine go hand in hand; they are deeply intertwined. The balance of the two together strengthens my connection to the land.'*

Chene Vineyard is truly remarkable, with Chardonnay and Gina's beloved Pinot Noir vines tiptoeing on the edge of the hill, sloping down the valley that leads to the Pacific just six kilometres away. The Edna Valley is framed by the Santa Luis mountain range, and the cool Pacific breeze flows into the valley, ideal for the cultivation of Chardonnay, Pinot Noir, Sauvignon Blanc, and Aligoté, the last of which Gina hopes to graft into the vineyard next year. It's not common to find artisans working in Edna, the majority of which is farmed conventionally on the valley floor and sold to corporate giant Gallo. *'We stick out like a sore thumb in our area,'* Gina revealed earlier this year during a visit to London. *'We've been certified biodynamic since 2020, and our vineyards look completely different to those around us. We grow wildflowers, native grasses, and cover crops. Some people think we're insane for growing anything but the vines in*

the vineyard, but to us, it's crazy not to. Soil is the stomach of any agricultural land, and its microbial terroir is its heartbeat. If you have life in the vineyard, you have life in the wine. We have 12,000 vines and it's like seeing all of them as 12,000 dots in the bigger picture.'

Natural wine-growing is a somewhat nuanced topic, particularly concerning what is permitted in the vineyards versus what is right for each specific piece of land. Gina eschews spraying copper and sulphur in her vineyards, elements technically permitted in biodynamic farming. *'We only use natural products,'* she explains. *'We use nettles and horsetail, which have high levels of natural sulphur; we make these into teas and spray in the spring. The nettles grow in at the edge of the vineyard, and the horsetail grows on the riverbed next door. We also use cinnamon oil, which sticks to the vine's leaves and prevents fungal diseases from spreading. We make our own compost using manure – from next door's farm, all the pomace from the grapes, and the lees from the winemaking process – which we keep insulated and then apply in winter to every other row. Making it ourselves is a great way to utilize our waste streams: our green waste, our pomace from the winery, manure, etc. This gives us an outlet to recycle carbon while using high-quality ingredients that we can source on our* own to make high-quality compost material. It's a lot like cooking: in the end, there's nothing better than a home-cooked meal.'

The wines Gina makes under the Lady of the Sunshine label are a bewitching play on flavour and dimension, and are the initial impetus for my trip out to California and down to the SLO Coast that late August afternoon. Contrary to the often laissez-faire attitude of some natural winemakers, Gina's attention to detail and curation of texture in the cellar is palpable. True to one of the pillars of natural winemaking, she allows her wines to ferment with native yeasts in the winery, resulting in a flinty, saline character, which Gina says brings tension and structure without any tweaks. She also uses skin contact and lees contact to build layers within the wine; and has even started a solera – a one-off barrel in which she collects portions of wine from each year and blends them together – another useful tool in building natural wines with depth. True to her biodynamic roots, she works with the lunar calendar to ensure the wine is bottled or moved when the moon is pulling down, so the wine is settled, which she is able to plan a year in advance.

As we wander through Mountain Meadow, an impossibly tranquil Pinot Noir vineyard off the highway that she and Mikey have recently

started farming, I ask Gina what really drives her quest for farming and winemaking the way she does.

'For me, biodynamics is a holistic style of regenerative farming that connects us back to the natural rhythm of Mother Nature. It connects to the seasonal transitions, to the moon, to the land, to the soil, and to the people. Over time, we have lost our original human connection to the land through industrialized agriculture and the need to control, organize, and dominate nature. But what happens when we begin to observe, listen, and learn from the land again? What happens when we shift our perspective to see the farm as one living organism, one body? What happens when we let nature find its rhythm again, when we let go and listen? We can become a tool that helps maintain balance. We can continue to evolve and share these ideas, then take root once again. We can restore that original connection to the land, and when that happens, the rhythm grows louder, and we find we are not so different from Mother Nature after all. The body and the land mirror each other, and, one day, our bodies will go back to the land. After us, what will be left is the land for the next generations. How do we want to be remembered?'

THE HEIRESS OF ETNA – a mountain's future hope

SONIA GAMBINO, GUSTINELLA

'If I'd had the time to stop and think about what was happening, I likely wouldn't have done it,' Sonia Gambino ruminates as we stand in her small 'garage' winery, Gustinella, on Mount Etna on a spring morning in April.

The room we are standing in is really, in fact, a garage, or at least that was the original idea before Sonia's parents left Maletto, the minute village – the highest on Etna – and headed up north. As it happened, Sonia was born in Milan. After a degree in Gastronomic Sciences and a Masters in Viticulture and Enology, Sonia eventually worked her way back down to Sicily and landed a job in Marsala on the western side of the island. But then, 2020 came knocking, and the world locked down. Overnight, Sonia found herself in her parents' unfinished house in Maletto, completely alone, waiting for the earliest opportunity to leave.

'When I first arrived, the locals would just stare at me,' Sonia recalls. 'I didn't blame them; imagine such a small, sleepy town full of elderly residents, and then one day, a young woman appears without warning.' Sonia did her best to distract herself over the first few months by growing vegetables in the small garden beside the house. Eventually, an elderly man stopped by to look at her vegetables. 'Don Vincenzo!' Sonia remembers. 'He kept coming to lean over the fence and offer me gardening advice. Then,

one day, he told me he had something to show me. He took me up to this tiny vineyard high above the village; it's 1,200 metres above sea level, and from it you can see Etna's peak in the near distance. It was more like a big garden, but full of these old vines, and each was so different from one to the next. Don Vincenzo told me he was too old to farm it.'

To Sonia, it felt like a door had opened. She'd wanted to escape the tiny, forgotten village of her ancestors, but now she'd seen a glimmer of something that could alter the trajectory of her life. 'I asked Don Vincenzo if I could do a little experiment with his vineyard and try to make some wine. He told me, "As long as you make me 365 litres from it because I drink a litre every day!"'

Sonia told Don Vincenzo he had a deal. The first step of the was to clear a corner of the garage for a winery. But things were developing fast around her. 'The day I made the deal with Don Vincenzo, the whole village knew about it. Of course, what did I expect? When I came back to the house, I ran into a queue of villagers all asking me, "Are you the daughter of Gustinello?" Gustinello was my grandfather's village nickname. They told me that my grandfather used to own the village palmento – a sort of Sicilian local winery where families would go and make their wine. Growing up, I knew he was involved in this, but

Wine to try: Vina di Confine (Gustinella – Sicily, Italy)

I had no idea that it was so big and so important to all these people.'
One by one, the villagers took Sonia to their vineyards, a miscellany of tiny plots saturated with old, mysterious vines; nut, cherry, and olive trees; wildflowers and fauna that had never seen as much as a whiff of chemical input.

As with Don Vincenzo, all these neighbours were too old to tend the plots them themselves, and without a generation beneath to hand over to, they sat idle. '*I thought to myself, "I've really stumbled upon something incredible here." That year, instead of making 300 litres, I made 3,000.*'

By the end of that first year, there was really no turning back for Sonia and her 'little experiment'. The corner of the garage had, within two months, become a full winery. That first harvest, Sonia fell in love with a pistachio farmer, and by the beginning of her second harvest, they had welcomed their daughter, Emma. '*Everything moved so fast!*' she remembers. Things moved so fast that Sonia found herself making wine from varieties she hadn't had the chance to identify, but the truth is no one knows what some of them are. The reason for this detail lies in Sicily's layered history. '*We know the Greeks brought Grenache here,*' she says, '*but even my Grenache is so different from the Grenache in neighbouring towns.*'

'During the early nineteenth century, a British admiral called Nelson was placed on Etna and tasked with creating a wine region with the same international acclaim as other Sicilian regions like Marsala, but they planted varieties that weren't suited to the altitude and cool temperatures of Maletto. The project failed and the locals went back to their old varieties, taking cuttings from vines nearby. That explains why these old vines today have so much genetic diversity. And that is why I'm so interested in all these varieties – lost and long forgotten by the rest of the mountain. I need to find out what they are and preserve them.'

The varieties of which Sonia is certain include Grenache and Alicante Bouschet (which is fascinatingly pink throughout), hyper-local varieties Minella, Grecanico Dorato, and Albanello. There is also Trebbiano – 'I have no idea how that got here,' Sonia shrugs – Moscatella, and a small scattering of Sicilian staples, Nerello Mascalese and Carricante, which often struggle to ripen at 1,000 metres and above, but perform well in Sonia's blends.

As for the rest, Sonia is working with an ampelographer to try and fill in the gaps. She wants to take cuttings and replant them to ensure these ancient varieties have a place in Etna's contemporary future. The villagers are, of course, thrilled with all the activity, and the fact that Sonia is rebuilding a part of Etna's history that might have otherwise been abandoned as is often the fate of the world's rural landscapes.

'The villagers really appreciate what I'm doing, they are always trying to help, stopping by to tell me, "this vineyard is looking good, this one looks ready to pick, this wall needs replacing", and so on! There is a guy in his nineties, he's still working, still so active. Once I called him and said, "Donino, do you remember I told you about the work I'm doing with Grenache selections?" He said, "Sonia, you have a terrible memory! You told me that three months ago, I've already made a hundred cuttings for you!"'

Out of all the world's wine-growing regions, this is a joyously simple place to grow and make natural wine. The vines – which have never seen any chemical intervention – thrive at the altitude and the pressures that plague other areas are non-existent here, dramatically reducing the need for even natural sprays. The snow from the cap of Etna keeps the vines hydrated during the growing season, and a constant layer of cover crop works to keep the topsoil active, requiring only a quick mow from time to time. Phylloxera has never been a risk here, also thanks to the altitude and sandy soils, which the pest seems to avoid like the plague (*pun intended and delivered*). All the old vineyards in the highest altitudes around the village are ungrafted. *'These old plants are so strong, so resilient. These aren't monoculture vineyards. It's a healthy system that has just worked for the hundred years these vines have been alive, and likely centuries more.'*

In the winery, I jolt back to life as, out of the corner of my eye, I see my three-year-old son Leonard try to twist open a concrete tank that is full of wine that will soon be ready for bottling. *'The next generation!'* Sonia laughs, *'My daughter is the same, always trying to open everything.'*

I look around at the winery equipment, there isn't a barrel in sight. *'I'm not ready to use wood,'* Sonia tells me. *'I'm still learning the vines, the terroir, what it tastes like, what it can do. I want to focus on concrete and glass, glass in particular translates the purity of mountain wines.'*

No chemicals are used at any stage until bottling when a tiny dose of sulphites is sometimes added, although in such a tiny amount that Sonia is not required to add 'Contains Sulphites' on her labels, a very rare occurrence to say the least.

I ask her about the wines and how she decides what her bottlings will be. *'Don Vincenzo's vineyard, I always keep separate. It's a special project,*

the one that changed my life. The rest I blend.'

'It's hard work farming and maintaining all these tiny parcels, but, of course, it's worth it. It's a big work, but one that's important for my grandfather's region. For my region.'

The wines we taste from tank and bottle are lifted and fine, reflecting the coolness of the mountain, but also the care that has been taken in making them.

'If I'd had the time to stop and think about what was happening, I likely wouldn't have done it. But, looking back,' she adds, *'it was my destiny.'*

GUT OGGAU,
ROOT TIME

It's a Friday in May and the rain pelts demonically on the windows of my train carriage as it twists through the Austrian landscape outside of Vienna. In about five minutes, I will realize I'm on the wrong train and will have to stand in the torrent for fifteen minutes before I can board another train back, this time the correct way around the enormous lake of Neusiedl, to my destination. Life, it seems, is mocking me, and perhaps I deserve it for all the #andbreathe selfies I've been posting on my Instagram stories from the comfort of the (incorrect) train. Rain seeps into my left sock.

I've come to Austria not to take selfies, in fact, I've come to get as far away from my materialistic urban-ness as I possibly can. I'm here to get my hands dirty – really, properly dirty – over two days, learning both the theory and practical realities of biodynamic wine-growing at winery Gut Oggau's inaugural course: Root Time. Defined as 'the study of dynamics in living systems' (bio = life, dynamic = energy), when applied to wine-growing, biodynamics focuses on the vineyard as an entire ecosystem as opposed to isolating the vine. It also acknowledges the role of cosmic rhythms and how they affect both the growth of a vine and the taste of the final wine made from it. Habitually dismissed by its detractors as a little too far-fetched and spiritual, the concept of biodynamics is that everything on the planet is living and gives off some sort of energy. The faces behind Gut Oggau – Stephanie and Eduard Tscheppe – have long been unyielding devotees of the biodynamic method, even sitting on the board of its global governing body Demeter.

I've known of biodynamics for years; many of my wine lists contain a high percentage of biodynamic wines, and compared to other wines, they don't necessarily *taste* different, rather they give the impression of being authentic and self-assured, like that friend in the group who has somehow just always been themselves and is not at all phased that mullets are back.

'We've been biodynamic since day one in 2007,' Eduard corrects me as I frantically scribble into my notebook. *'For us, it has always been the most important element of what we do.'* Of course, here in Burgenland, we are in the global heartland of the biodynamics ideology, its key architect Rudolf Steiner was Austrian, too, and I get the sense that Austrians see the method as more rational and less esoteric and 'space-hippie' than others might. My theory certainly checks out here.

It's hard to overstate the influence Gut Oggau has had in the world of natural wine over the last decade.

With two of the movement's contemporary figureheads, and exporting to more than sixty countries worldwide, if you glance through the windows of any of the world's best natural-wine shops and bars, you will likely see one of the Gut Oggau family members peering down at you from a shelf or emerging on your Instagram feed. I've visited the winery numerous times over the last ten years and have always been struck by Stephanie and Eduard's complete confidence in what they are doing. The wines they produce are animated, intense, and somehow intellectual; they reflect the duo well.

Each wine, or family member from three generations depicted on Gut Oggau's label, correlates to certain vineyard plots, characteristics, and 'personalities' in the soil. The grandparent generation: Mechthild, Bertholdi, and the parent generation Emmeram, Joshuari and Cecilia, among others – are planted on slopes on a mix of slate and limestone, revealing 'relaxed and mature' qualities; while the young generation – Atanasius, Theodora, and Winifred – are planted on lower, flatter vineyards of gravel and limestone, giving them the zest and yield associated with youth. It seems like a sort of Austrian *Encanto*, if the Madrigal family were in fact vine plots of Weissburgunder, Grüner Veltliner, Welschriesling, Blaufränkisch, Zweigelt, and Roesler.

The winemaking is the simple part, and Gut Oggau takes a chef's approach: good ingredients = little interference needed. *'People focus so much time talking about what they do in the cellar; we need to focus on what's happening in the vineyard,'* Stephanie says to me as we ride our electric bikes through the soft and verdant spring landscape on the first morning of Root Time. Fortunately, the rain has decided to take a break, which is a relief as we will be outside for most of the day, and my sock isn't yet dry. Stephanie looks to the sky. *'We really needed this,'* she laments. *'Normally, we rely on rain in winter to carry the vines through the growing season, but this year it never came.'* I think of Lake Neusiedl, which provides a crucial presence to the vineyards planted on the slopes all around, and wonder how many years of no rain it would take to dry out altogether. *'Many of the region's old "Premier Cru" sites planted have become too hot. We're lucky to be closer to the mountain and a little cooler.'*

The first morning of Root Time starts with a walk through the vineyard that contributes towards the Eugenie cuvée. Despite the weather, everyone is in good spirits. It's amazing how unwaveringly upbeat people can be at the thought of wine with lunch. The area on which we're stood is a seven-million-year-old mussel bed that over the millennia has given way to layers of clay-silica soils. Clay is a particularly useful ally these days when you stop to consider the rising temperatures and worrying lack of water in much of the world's key wine-growing regions. Clay can absorb water and hold it for when the vine needs it the most during the growing season. *'We're only planting vineyards on clay now, it's a way of future-proofing our work.'* There is another benefit to clay, something I would have never imagined. *'Clay is a connector of the cosmos,'* says Eduard, *'it is sensitive to movements in the cosmos and connects the vines to their rhythms.'* In the vineyard we're encouraged to dig our hands into the soil and lift-up big scoops to our noses to smell. *'Smelling soil releases oxytocin into your blood stream,'* says Eduard, *'it creates the same chemical reaction as hugging your mother.'* It's a beautiful sentiment, and in following the instruction something like relief washes over me as I breathe in the wet, dark earth.

We turn to shoot thinning, the process of removing shoots that are unlikely to bear fruit to prioritize those that likely will over the coming season. The redundant shoots are collected in baskets and will reappear later to accompany our late-afternoon wine tasting, by this time transformed into unbearably delicious fried snacks, doused in salt and sharp, sweet vinegar. It feels good to be close to the ground despite the perpetual drizzle. The soil underneath me feels soft, and spongy. I ask Eduard if the texture is of significance. *'Spongy soil can store more water and microbes,'* he begins. *'The colour is significant, too. The darker the soil, the richer the humus. Rich humus works to bind carbon dioxide and allows the vines to thrive, as well as supporting life under the surface. Healthy soil is highly populated soil. There are eight billion creatures working backstage under the surface, if you count insects, mycelia, bacteria, and microbes. Without backstage, there can be no concert.'*

I think of all the worrying statistics about dwindling insect populations I read, and ask what can be done to encourage richer humus to develop in the vineyard. *'Take a look at all the plants around in the vines,'* Stephanie says. *'This vineyard is about so much more than just the vines themselves. We grow buckwheat, mustard, chickweed, peas, wheat, clover, and oil radishes; they compose our cover crop. Their growth creates oxygen in the soil and supports life under the vine.'* While cover crops aren't a particular focus of biodynamic farming, the role they play is an important one by strengthening biodiversity in an area and creating the wider ecosystem that Steiner referred to in his lectures. *'We also want to attract flying insects, as they transport the energy of the cosmos. Using insecticides in farming disrupts*

the natural balance of insect life, the effects of which we still don't fully understand.'

After lunch we cycle to a vineyard sloping gently downwards towards Neusiedl, which contributes its efforts into cuvée Cecilia. Here we spend the afternoon creating a biodynamic preparation named #500, a mix of cow manure, which has spent the previous winter buried underground in a cow horn, with water. At the crux of the theory behind the application is vitalizer: a dose sprayed onto the soil provides a high activation of soil life and the germination of seeds in the topsoil. We take it in turns to blend the manure together with water, using our arms to create a vortex effect in the liquid for an hour – 'dynamizing' the mixture.

It occurs to me that for years I have read about biodynamic preparations, and how they are made, but it's never occurred to me to ask why the application and its method is so important to biodynamic growers. Why cow horns? Why the need for a vortex? Does it need to be applied at a specific time? *'Cows are the sacred animals, that much has been observed by communities around the world for centuries,'* Eduard begins, *'their horns act like antenna for cosmic energy, giving the preparation a super-charge. The vortex we create mimics the spirals of the cosmos, allowing* further activation of the material. The process involves the matter itself, the human energy of the dynamizer, and the cosmic energy around. We apply it during favourable lunar constellations, when the soil is most receptive to the information.'* In the case of preparation #500, it is proven to fuel the soil's activity and rebalance its pH levels while increasing the depth of the vines' root systems. *'The roots are a vine's nutrient larder, Darwin also conceived that plants and trees think through their roots, essentially making a plant's roots its brain. But more than that, it is also the part of the vine that gives a wine its "sense of place" or "terroir". If we worked conventionally, we would spray commercial fertilizers that focus on the growth of the plant above the soil, and not on the roots.'* In other words, the wine could be from just about anywhere. It's an affirming notion, and a meditative experience walking up and down the vines with a small tank on my back, spraying the vines using a manual pump and sharing stories with my fellow Root Time sign-ups, who among them include France's first female Master of Wine Isabelle Legeron.

Later on during a well-earned run down of Gut Oggau wines, the topic moves from the vineyard to the cellar. Do cosmic activities play a role in the winemaking, too? Here, Stephanie and Eduard default to the biodynamic calendar created by Maria Thun. It seems straightforward enough if you have your act together. On 'fruit days', the wine is open and stable enough to be moved, so if a transfer of the wine is needed, or it's time to bottle the wine, that's when it will be carried out. On 'root days', the wine is more closed, so should be left to rest. The finished wines taste more harmonious, and happier in who they are, when handled at the right time.

Over dinner that evening, I try and distil the learnings of the day. Something is irking me... what little thought I've given such apparent colossal influences of the cosmos on life on earth; how little I've been told about it until now. We accept notions like tides, and that people tend to go a bit doolally on the night of a full moon, but it more or less ends there. *'People have become disconnected from their instincts,'* Isabelle says next to me. She's right, and I ask myself why. I move to pick up my phone for a quick doom scroll and ask myself if in doing so, would I be feeding my surface or my roots? There is so much more to learn, and, in so many ways, it seems we have only scratched the surface.

'Everything is connected,' Eduard summarizes. *'In the end nature has a way of rebalancing itself, but for us, biodynamic farming is about helping to regenerate the earth, to rebuild the resources we have taken from it. Sustainability is a term that has fallen prey to greenwashing, and allows companies to avoid commitment, but to us it means "to make something living more alive". That's the true sentiment of what we're doing. We live by "The Honourable Harvest" and just take what we need and leave the rest for the next generations. We farmers are the curators of our land, and the wines that we produce from our vines can stand the test of time. Viticultural products can travel and tell their story all over the world. Tell the story of a piece of earth, and a particular time. For us, there is no such thing as a bad vintage, some might be intense in ways, but we rely on healthy grapes, and our vineyards don't let us down. We don't always get everything right, but to quote Samuel Beckett: "Try again. Fail again. Fail better".'*

The next day, we drive to a field that Stephanie and Eduard have recently purchased, which they will over time make into a forest, bringing with it even more biodiversity to its surroundings. Together we plant a cherry tree. It occurs to me that for all their learnings over the last seventeen years, the team at Gut Oggau must feel like they are just scratching their surface, too. *'For us, it's not just about finding the truth, but more the search for the truth. It's not just what can we do, but who do we ultimately want to be?'*

Wine to try: Josephine (Gut Oggau – Burgenland, Austria)

THE EPICUREAN – on natural wine's front line

MARGAUX
AUBRY

Margaux Aubry knows her way around a good wine list. Born in Lyon, Margaux made her way over to London in 2010, immersing herself in the centre of London's then embryonic natural-wine sphere: restaurant Terroirs, owned by natural-wine importers Les Caves de Pyrene (see page 58).

'I went to Terroirs a lot in 2012 before I worked there. I sat at the bar one afternoon and ordered Domaine Ganevat's J'en Veux from Jura. The first sips gave me goosebumps; actual tears came to my eyes. That experience changed everything. I started to wonder how it was even possible to drink a bottle of wine without asking yourself where it came from, who made it, and the story behind it. I worked for over a year and a half at Terroirs and had the chance to meet so many winemakers between RAW (see page 111), the Real Wine Fair, and wine trips with suppliers. I learned so much and had my mind blown a good dozen times. Working at Terroirs changed my heart, palate, and overall vision of wines and the importance of how they are made. I became thirsty with an insatiable soif!'

In 2014, she and her to-be business partner Joe Sharratt stumbled upon an old kebab house on Brixton's Water Lane, which they transformed into one of the city's most beloved wine bistros, Naughty Piglets. I love this spot, and with every visit

I am left feeling utterly replete, not to mention waxing lyrical at the top of my lungs about a new liquid discovery thanks to Margaux's cleverly curated cellar.

'Building a strong cellar of wines made by friends was always the main focus when opening Naughty Piglets. Having built strong relationships with suppliers throughout the years, I got my hands on yearly allocations and started ordering too much! I work emotionally. I never ever structure a wine list in a way that can be explained other than how I feel about a producer and her or his wines. Perhaps my only rule was to list winemakers I had met or visited – to be able to speak anecdotally and personally when pouring their wines. A few winemakers have become close friends, and I could spend all day listening to their savoir-faire, their beliefs; how they beat viruses, hail, frost; how to treat, plough, understand the terroir; the bemoaning their conventional neighbours, why they think she/he is doing the wrong thing; the ongoing gossip and so forth, I love it!'

Naughty Piglets is forever heaving and for good reason. Margaux not only curates her list from the heart, but she knows how to approach each guest and find a natural wine for each taste. *'When I started Naughty Piglets almost ten years ago, my guests fell into camps. There were* those who were already convinced, the connoisseurs, or I should say those who thought they were connoisseurs, the sceptics, and the ANTI. Particularly over the past five years, the demand for natural wines has gone crazy, which has a lot to do with social media. I reckon a third were drinking it because it was cool, the other third were really getting into it for what it represents, and the others were clearly still ANTI. I used to feel angry or frustrated when people drank it just to follow a trend, but at the end of the day, it meant more and more people wanted a wine with a real story, made with sweat, respect, and real care.'

'I think a story I will never forget is the night Jay Rayner turned up with his wife on their way to our neighbour's opening night. As a food critic, he is famous for his disdain for natural wines, I was naturally intimidated, but the challenge excited me. I poured them Jean Maupertuis Puy Long 2014, a simple but very drinkable Chardonnay from Auvergne. I was assertive as I just loved the wines. When he left, he tweeted, "Thanks to Margaux at Naughty Piglets who served me a natural wine I liked", to his 300,000 followers. That was it – legend!'

I ask Margaux if there is a pairing she particularly remembers from over the years at Naughty Piglets. 'I adored serving a cuvée called Far-Ouest by Domaine Mylène Bru (a glorious winemaker from Languedoc-Roussillon) with our barbeque pork belly and Korean spice. It's a blend of Cinsault, Syrah, Carignan, and Grenache. You smell the garrigue and the delicate spices in the wine, and they dance with the fat and the gochujang in the dish. Or cuvée Diables by Amós Bañeres with a coffee crème caramel; a boiled-sweet Macabeo aged for three months in old oak. Heaven,' she sighs.

I ask her what could be done to convince more people to embrace natural wines as, clearly, they have so much to offer.

'I think sommeliers need more experience, something that is getting better as time goes on and natural wine is more universally served. A lot of wine-lovers who fall into the ANTI category are there because they have had a bad experience from a sommelier who is poorly trained or doesn't have that much experience. There is so much nuance in natural wines, it takes someone who really cares for both the wine and people to serve them both properly.'

Wine to try: Chardonnay En Chalasse (Domaine Labet – Jura, France)

MARGAUX AUBRY

SOUS VOILE

'*We are not missing this shit for* anything,' says Anders. It's summer in Copenhagen and I find myself short of breath trying to keep up with a flock of sommeliers who are racing towards the harbour. Anders is the chef at the city's beloved wine bar Den Vandrette, and for wine, and wine only, he moves at this kind of speed. In my hand, a sword. I laugh, if this was home in London, I'd get seven years behind bars for carrying a penknife without good explanation, and yet here I am running through a swarm of summer tourists with a sword and, as yet, no real way of explaining what the hell it is I am doing. Someone darts ahead of me, grasping a bottle of Charles Dufour Champagne by the neck. Another overtakes with a Georgian drinking horn in hand. Our group sprints up Copenhagen's newly completed harbour bridge, and comes to a stop, facing out towards the sea.

It's an extraordinary sight. Nordlys, the world's oldest active cargo ship, laden with 10,000 bottles of natural wine, is being gently guided into the city's waterways. The sails are down and the crew is gathered at the front of the ship. We can see them clearly now, from the bridge where we stand as we crane our necks down towards this celestial sight. Sune Rosforth, founder of wine-import company Rosforth & Rosforth, and his kids are visible from the ship's bow. They are all waving at us; I'm pretty sure I can hear singing, too. Someone hands me the Champagne and I swiftly lob off the top with the sword, something I've only just learned how to do (but which thankfully goes off without a hitch). The cork bounds into the water as the ship passes through the bridge underneath us. We fill the horn with Champagne and take it in turns to drink until the bottle is drained.

Once they've docked, the rest of the day is spent unloading the cargo from within Nordlys hold. We form an assembly line. Case by case, the wine is lifted out and placed onto trestle tables on which we slice open the boxes and painstakingly label every one of the 10,000 bottles with a sticker emblazoned with the words 'Fair Transport, Cargo

Under Sail'. It's a warm day in the city, and we soon begin to flag. We're in luck. Before long, bottles from Sune's stash (he conveniently stores his imports directly at the harbour) are siphoned off and shared amongst the motley crew who have amassed to help out. I share a *Chin Chin* with a famous Danish opera singer over a sip of Baptiste Cousin's electric Grolleau, I raise a *Skål* to a noma sommelier over a glug of La Lune Chenin Blanc by Mark Angeli, and reach over to clink my glass of Toby Bainbridge's Highway 8 with the ship's captain, Anne-Flore. This will be her first drink since setting sail from France and I can tell by her expression that she might need a top up.

Her crew by now have their feet on terra firma and have laced themselves among the crowd of us land-bound mortals, keen to keep their glasses full and understandably after such a long hiatus – all booze is banned while at sea. I peer around at them in shy fascination. Despite the rather bohemian air of the auxiliaries, the sailors remain remarkably conspicuous. Broad smiles sit atop sun-weathered faces and masses of salt-matted locks that look like they'd be painful to untangle. I have a word with myself for being such a square and turn back to Anne-Flore.

She tells me that the winds have been strong and they have made good time on their voyage – neither factor is guaranteed when you are the captain of a ship without a motor. In fact, little is certain when you are sailing a ship made in 1873 that was dredged up from the seabed in the Netherlands and purchased for one euro by a trio of friends just over a decade ago. A few glasses deep, I find out Nordlys is one of two sail-powered vessels in the fleet of Tres Hombres, a company devoted to the dream of creating a sustainable shipping movement.

The other ship, also called Tres Hombres, borrows its hull from a German torpedo boat built in 1924 and used in the Second World War. It's then that Anne-Flore casually throws in that she actually mastered in fashion, but ended

up as a ship captain due to a proclivity for wood. All these
flecks of information seem so wholly inconceivable that
I find myself repeating them to make sure I've heard
right and that my glass of Chenin isn't tricking my ears
into hyperbole.

It was 2008 when Anjou natural winemaker Olivier
Cousin waved goodbye to his harvest interns as they set
off for the French coastal town of Brest, clasping between
them the dream to find a ship and hitch-hike the Atlantic.
They were in luck: Tres Hombres, the ship, arrived a few
days into their search. The interns negotiated being taken
on as sailing apprentices, and the crew embarked on their
voyage. News of the unusual feat soon reached back to
Anjou. Olivier, himself a retired skipper, tracked down
Tres Hombres and began hatching a plan to sail his wines
to his importer in New York. Other natural winemakers
were keen to join the experiment: Mark Angeli, Michel and
Beatrice Augé, Julie and Toby Bainbridge, Guy Bossard,
Thierry Michon, and Philippe Tessier, were among the
inaugural sign-ups; each committing a few hundred
bottles to the seminal junket. Tres Hombres set sail.
However, upon arriving in New York, the ship was unable
to dock and it became clear that they would have to turn
around. With a ship still encumbered with wine, Olivier
was forced to look for other solutions.

'Olivier called me,' Sune recollects. 'He said there was a sail-
powered ship full of wine crossing back across the Atlantic
and would I be interested?' I eye Sune curiously. 'You know
what I said?' I do, but I want to hear him say it. And here,
he grins nostalgically, and delivers the two words I have
come to associate as synonymous with Sune in the years
that have passed since we first met: 'Let's go!' The annual
arrival of the ships to Copenhagen is now woven so tightly
into the cultural fabric of the city that you could mistake it
for folklore. And Sune plays his role in the mystique with
aplomb aplenty. Credited for persuading René Redzepi
and then sommelier Pontus Elofsson to ditch classic wine
at noma, Denmark's natural wine potentate has since been

gradually imbuing the country's every orifice with bottles that he loves, seemingly entirely without ego or pretence. One such wine is L'Atlantique, from a single barrel of Olivier's Le Franc Cabernet Franc cuvée that was loaded onto Tres Hombres and assumed the part of a stowaway, journeying with the ship to her other destinations before landing in Copenhagen to be bottled. Originally from Olivier's old-vine parcels, the wine had been in barrel for two years, then in bottle for two more, but it was not tasting right: it lacked maturity, balance, a sense of itself. Unable to identify why, Olivier began to wonder if a sea voyage would give the wine something the land couldn't. I reflect with Sune over a shared bottle of L'Atlantique 2012. The wine tastes rugged and contemplative, yet undeniably complete.

For Sune, it's clear: after the journey by sea, the wines become settled, more at ease. These aren't words Sune uses, of course. Sune seldom uses words when feelings flow in such abundance. Instead, he pauses, often just long enough for me to start to fidget awkwardly as if I'd asked a stupid question. *'If you see wine as a living thing then you understand that these wines have been on a big adventure,'* he muses. And there end the words. I let the feeling wash over me and I have to say, it feels pretty good.

It's 10.15am and I've blown it. I had come to wave goodbye to Tres Hombres for another year and she's already gone. I had more questions to ask Anne-Flore. I heard that Jakob, the Danish opera singer, was there to sing the ship away. I stand sullenly by the water. Sune appears behind me: *'Spencer, if you're quick, maybe you can catch her pass by the summerhouse in Snekkersten. They're headed that way.'* He's referring to a town up north by the Swedish border. It seems like a lot of effort to only have a chance at glimpsing a boat on the horizon. Len, my six-month old is peering up at me from his stroller. I have shit to do. I can't go off chasing a ship. But here comes that feeling again, visceral and fidgety. I think of that first year and the desperate sprint to the harbour. I think of the bottle of

Charles Dufour's Champagne and the sword. I'm on the train now and I can see from the ship's GPS tracker that we're roughly head to head en route to Snekkersten. The train conductor announces that we have slowed down due to a broken-down train in front of us. I'm feeling short of breath again. We pull into the station and I race down the hill to the beach, trying not to wake the sleeping baby who is strapped to my front. Sune's wife, Veronica, and their kids are already on the pier. *'You've just missed her,'* Veronica reports, handing me her binoculars. I'm gutted, I could've sworn we'd taken the lead a few stops back.

'Wait, look! She's turning back towards us!' Alberto yells from ahead of us. And he's right; I look through the binoculars and Tres Hombres is facing us down. The sails are up now, but I can see the movement of arms, waving at us from the front. I laugh: if this was home in London, none of it would work. These scenes would get lost in the noise of the city and the magic would be lessened somehow, polluted or forgotten. But here, it all fits. Olivier and Sune's vision has a home and Copenhagen is richer for it. I face out towards the sea, and I wave back.

how to
ENJOY
NATURAL
WINE

How to buy natural wine

Buying any kind of wine can be intimidating. By its nature, wine is expensive – it's an investment. It's not solely the costs of a wine-grower cultivating the grapes and making the wine; that wine is then often stored, transported, and taxed when it reaches its destination. In the UK, a bottle of wine, made responsibly, will now cost you upwards of £11 ($13) in a shop and £30 ($36) in a restaurant.

Wine, particularly natural wine, is about trust. Trust in the wine-grower that they have made their wine from healthy, scrupulously selected grapes. Trust in the distributor or importer that they have transported and stored the wine in a way that preserves its condition and detail. Trust in the retailer that this bottle really deserves a place on the shelf or a venue's wine list – and that it fits in with their ethos, which you by now also trust.

The best advice I can give on choosing the right wine is to find a wine person who understands your palate. I've served guests for twenty years, and nearly fifteen have been through the lens of wine. I can't tell you how important it is for me to find the right wine to suit each of my guest's (unbelievably diverse) tastes. Sure, not all retailers and sommeliers are hard-wired that way, but all you need to do is find someone you trust with your inclinations and stick to them like glue. They will remember your likes, loathes, and 'mehs'. They will go out of their way to find you the best possible bottle for your buck and might even find a way to offer you a discount so you can try something special if it falls outside of your budget.

Find the right natural wine bottle to fit your vibe...

In the absence of a vinous god or goddess who understands your palate, here are a few tips to find the best natural wine bottle for you.

1. Play distributor bingo
This is my favourite. The world of wine has changed a lot in recent years, no part as much as the distributor sector. The waning trend for larger distributors has made room for smaller, highly creative enterprises – many of which have a particular niche or overarching 'feel' to their wines. If you drink a bottle you love, it's worth finding out who imported or distributed it and finding others by the same company – chances are you will find a trend in the kind of wines you love.

2. Be upfront about price
There is nothing new about this advice, and it is not limited to natural wines, but it perpetually bears repeating. Figure out how much you want to spend on a bottle and be upfront about it with the retailer or sommelier. These people have dedicated their working hours to sharing their love of wines and they will rise to the challenge of finding you the best possible wine for your budget. Plus, if you are on a date and feel awkward about stating your price, know that it is actually pretty sexy to be with someone who knows their limits.

3. Label scrutiny
For a very long time wine labels were terribly traditional. And then things started to change. With younger generations taking over their family estates or starting their own, switching to organic or regenerative practices, labels edged towards the more upbeat and uninhibited. For a while, finding natural wines became easy; the labels became a calling card – a way for wine-growers to set themselves apart from the conventional.

Many winemakers have now started to mimic this style of label, making it hard to discern between natural and unnatural bottles. These wines could even be made with low intervention and taste on the natural side, but not from organic, biodynamic, or regeneratively farmed fruit, which is the main point. If you see one of these labels in a standard supermarket, it's usually safe to assume the wine isn't natural; strict supermarket criteria means natural wines don't often end up on their shelves.

4. Use your own language

Most people know the taste they want to experience when they sit down in a restaurant. Think of walking into your favourite cocktail bar and being able to describe the off-menu cocktail you fancy – once you've tried it a few times, there's no going back. Yet, when it comes to wine, there is a notion that we should possess an entirely different vocabulary. If we don't know every word of this illusory dictionary, no one will respect us, let alone be willing to give us a bottle of delicious wine to drink. Allow me to liberate you from this mundane and archaic mentality... You know how you want a wine to make you feel. Whether it be taste, texture, or a whole vibe, get comfortable describing wine in your own terms. Did you try a wine on holiday that tastes smoky and fierce, like Taylor Swift in her revenge era? Or a skin-contact wine that, while there was a hint of nectarine, reminded you almost entirely of cheese puffs? Maybe you don't want any umami or wildness in your wine today and you just want something reminiscent of fizzy strawberry laces. That is absolutely okay. Do you want a thinking wine? Or an easy guzzler to share with a group? It's okay to say you like natural wine but not when it tastes too much like cider; or that too much acidity gives you reflux. Any wine-lover who sells wine is all too familiar with these evocations and will rise to the task.

How to taste natural wine

My watershed moment in wine wasn't at the top of a mountain in New Zealand drinking Grand Cru Champagne (that did happen, but for the purposes of this chapter it would likely help if I didn't sound like a jumped-up twat). I had my first big moment with wine at my 18th birthday over a shared bottle of Pinot Grigio my dad had ordered for the table. The second cheapest white wine on the list and shared between what felt like thirty-five people.

I wish I could say I was brought up around wine; sadly despite my parents' somewhat Mediterranean outlook, wine rarely featured – especially after they cottoned onto my drinking directly from the bag in box as a pre-teen and moved my sources firmly out of reach. So, I grew up with alcohol very much under lock and key (although I did do a yearly inventory of my parents' cocktail cabinet, complete with impressive layers of dust – looking at you, 1981 Cointreau).

What I remember about this particular moment with the Pinot Grigio was how everything zeroed in when I tasted it. My senses felt heightened: my tongue identified texture (what precious little there is in a typical Northern Italian Pinot Grigio), then there was acid, mineral. My nose picked up a prickle of stone fruit and a salty lick of warm, wet stone. I was in a moment, completely absorbed in taste and smell – maybe only mirrored by a memory of long before, stuffing down raspberries in my grandad's garden with an air of catholic guilt while pretending to look after my little sister Miriam. I have a pretty pathetic attention span, but this moment forced me against my will to stop and forget the world around me.

When I finally (and totally accidentally) fell into the world of wine as a sommelier, I didn't find it hard to build up a mental library of taste and memory. All I had to do was stop and zero in. This becomes both easier and harder over

HOW TO TASTE NATURAL WINE

time. Easier as habits become second nature with repetition; reflexive, instinctive. But ever more complex as tastings turned into a career, the career turns into responsibilities, and before I knew it, I found myself in a freezing cellar in the Loire Valley attempting to hold a vintage camera, notepad, pen, and decent conversation in a foreign language, and not look like a clown in front of my team.

For those wanting to master the art of tasting wine, particularly natural wine, the only real answer is practice. Natural wines for all their wonder and mind-bending possibilities also tend to have one pretty frustrating trait for those trying to understand them: they are rarely formulaic. Of course, there are thousands of natural wines around the world that show what sommeliers would call 'typicity', which essentially means a wine will taste how you might expect this kind of wine made with this kind of grape from this kind of place. But not all natural wines are born or made equal.

When it comes to wines with clear typicity, there are handy rules to follow – clues to look for. Take any wine course in the world and you can learn those hacks. But often, natural wines don't play by those rules. And don't even get me started on blind tasting, which when conducted with natural wine is usually one fat exercise in ego obliteration. The best luck I've ever had in blind tasting natural wines is by repeatedly tasting the wines over months and years, and having a connection to the person who makes them. It sounds twee but if you've walked the vineyards, smelled an active ferment, or can remember the way the winemaker looks when he talks, you are more likely to be able to detect the wines without looking at the bottle. PS, extra points for knowing the name of the family dog/ploughing horse.

When it comes to building your own library of taste, everyone has their own methods, but here are a few hacks I have developed over the last decade.

Taste wine like the natural wine Yoda you are destined to be...

1. Keep a notepad with you for tasting wine
Make sure it's one big enough that it's not a faff to write in, but one small enough not to be a faff carrying around with you any time you taste.

2. Take a photo of the label
This is completely socially acceptable these days and if you are a visual person like me, you are likely more able to remember a label than a cuvée name. Make a folder for pictures of bottles that you can pull out when you need. I have different folders for fizz, white, red, skin-contact, and rosé. Bonus points for pics with manicured or even better, soil-stained nails. You've been visiting vineyards, power to you.

3. Smell + Taste
There are plenty of books that will tell you how to taste wine, so I won't add to the noise here. What I will say is when tasting natural wines, be prepared for a lot more than just fruit, oak, and forest floor. Many natural wines offer up so many more nuances in texture and flavour than come with conventional wines. A slight fizz from some leftover CO_2, aroma of a freshly struck match? How many layers of texture are there? Likely quite a few, some pronounced or detailed, others a little harder to reach. Salinity features a lot with natural wines, but what kind of salt? Sea salt flakes? Licking a wet rock on a beach kind of saltiness? If there is fruit, what kind of fruit is it? Is it a fresh apple, your nan's apple pie, or as a waiter said to me recently: 'A bit like those sliced apple packs you'd get as a kid in your lunch box that's beginning to go a bit brown'. Are you sure that's not a vegetable or herb instead? The more detail, the better for remembering the wine.

4. Ignore everyone else

Don't watch what other people are doing, or how effortless you think everyone else looks. I have some friends who can taste, chat, write notes, make jokes (in different languages), and remember every detail of a wine long after a tasting. I tend to shut out the world and zero in. I ask myself, what is this wine trying to tell me? Once I've got that figured out, I can go back to the noise.

5. Finally, do I like this wine?

Sometimes it's as simple as 'gross, no, not for me'. But ask yourself – is there a reason? Is the wine corked? Or do you not like it because it smells a bit like your ex after he took a shower? Is it that you find it challenging now, but maybe your palate will like it in the future. Maybe this is to be catalogued as a *maybe next time* wine. And if you like it, why do you like it? How is it similar to other wines I've tried that I also like? Does it have a similar saline etching, or flinty undertone that you've come across in the past?

6. And finally, stick to your guns

It would be horrifyingly boring if we all took to the same things in life, even wine. Natural wine, in particular, is a precious and finite resource, and if we all had the same palate, the majority of us would have to crawl back to pale ale.

How to pair natural wine

For wine quaffers and foodies alike, pairing food and wine delivers peak geek levels of delight. When I started working with wine in 2011, my favourite part of the job was creating pairings for my restaurant guests. Wine could be used to accentuate a particular flavour in a dish, its innate acidity used to draw out sweetness, or accentuate a spice tucked into a sauce. Wine was a condiment, and my cupboard was fully stocked. Or so I thought.

When I started working with natural wines, I was frankly flummoxed by the kaleidoscope of new flavours, textures, acidities, and depth and detail they offered. Natural wine is so much more than responsible agricultural practices; it is also about taste. And when it comes to food and wine pairing, there is little else more satisfying than using natural wines to deliver an exhilarating impact. I am so grateful to my friend and former colleague at Evelyn's Table, Aidan Monk, for his singular ability to put words to our internal monologue during the first few years of food and wine pairing together. Kanpai, Aidan!

Here are a few of my reflections on pairing food and natural wines over the years:

The flow
Typically wine is paired with food to accentuate elements of a dish or ingredient. The wine is static; the dish is evolving. With natural wine, the opposite is true. Natural wine is often constantly changing in the glass, offering an ever-changing experience. The first glass can be an entirely different experience from the last. This can be likened to getting to know a person over time: the first impression is not the same as the second, and world's away from the last. Learn how a particular wine evolves in the glass or throughout the bottle, then choose a dish you think would like to go on that road trip.

The verve
Natural wines are alive. They possess not only intrinsic vibrancy but also vibratory qualities. Their energy digs deep into the dishes they are matched with, shaking them down and giving both a tangible lift and direction.

The fifth taste and beyond
Natural wine is about so much more than fruit, acid, and tannin. Expect minerals, salt, and other savoury compounds like umami and even vegetable characteristics. Expect multiple layers of texture at any one time: smooth and raw, or juicy and dry. Cook or order a dish that offers as many dimensions as your natural wine.

The thrill
One of the biggest paybacks of serving natural wine in a restaurant setting or at a dinner party is that it keeps your diners awake and alert, as opposed to drowsy or, god forbid, *bored*. This can be attributed to a few factors. Regularly natural wines have lower abv. Not always, but often. Then there's the fact that natural wine has an almost guaranteed undertone of acidity (and range of), which keeps the tongue and mind alert throughout a meal. And then, of course, your diner might be so on edge about being served natural wine that they are rooted to the spot in fear, or anticipation (or both).

Pair wines according to the hero elements of your grub...

With all types of food-and-natural-wine pairing, it's very much about trial and error. Pick up any book on wine, follow the formulas, and enjoy life from the safety net. Or steady your sea legs and head off on a trip into the uncharted. Here are my pairing hacks.

1. Salt
Truly the world's eighth wonder, salt's transformative talents are particularly tangible when blended with wine. If you put a tiny pinch of salt on your tongue and take a swirl of any wine, you will notice how your wine becomes more open and richer, with more fruit. This often provides a crucial collaboration with conventionally made wines that are often filtered and in serious need of the added depths donated by a salty dish. Natural wines, by contrast, tend to possess manifold inbuilt layers, which, when fused with salt, become a multi-dimensional feast for the senses. Many natural wines also possess a 'saltiness' of their own, bringing out sweetness and richness in foods, adding even more layers of detail to the union. Suddenly your dry white tastes less like biting straight into a lemon and more like lemon meringue pie with Chantilly cream. Your rosé tastes richer and more detailed. Your skin-contact tastes gentler and deeper, and your tannic-laden powerhouse red turns into a big, open-hearted softy.

Try: Your favourite brand of salted crisps with Cati Ribot Cambuix from Mallorca.

2. Fat
If it's fair to say that wine needs salt, the opposite is true for fat. Fat needs wine. It craves it. It lays up at night thinking about it. When we eat fat, it tends to make itself at home and spreads out, coating the tongue, cheeks, and roof of our mouths. As a meal

progresses, layers of fat and flavour continue to form and deepen. Wine's innate acidity and/or tannin compounds work to break down fat and weigh in with refreshment. Fat combines particularly well with skin-contact whites whose tannins work through it whilst building flavour on top. Sparkling also works well. Pét-nats, with their lower pressure levels, create a soft, emollient effect on the palate, while higher pressure sparklings, such as Champagnes and crémant (try Crémants de Alsace, Jura, or Loire), clean up after the house party.

Try: Fish and chips and a glug of Tissot Crémant de Jura. A few slices of your favourite salami and Escoda-Sanahuja Els Bassots from Catalunya.

3. Spice
There are a few different ways of approaching spice in food. You can practise the fire-extinguisher flex: countering spice with broad wines with a creamy or lactic feel. Naturally, darker, unfiltered rosés and richer whites from warm regions or textural varieties work well to take the edge off the heat. The second option is to lean into the spice and choose a wine with tannin. Tannin elevates spice and works to highlight any nuances in the sauce. Again, skin-contact wines work well here – white to deliver power and a level of savoury or aromatic detail, or a dry red with high acid and tannin to heighten the fiery fervour.

Try: Drunken fried rice or jollof with Petr Koráb Saint Laurent from Moravia in the Czech Republic (red), or Clos du Tue-Bœuf Romorantin from the Loire Valley in France (white), or Mtsvane by Pheasant's Tears from Kakheti in Georgia (skin-contact).

4. Umami
With the reputation of being notoriously tetchy when it comes to finding the right partner, umami is found in ingredients like miso, pork, aged cheeses, and, of course, Marmite/Vegemite. It can't be blamed for being so hard to pin down: its salty depths and nuanced textural facets can easily be misunderstood. Plus, it isn't into monogamy.

Umami-heavy foods with the wrong wine can draw out bitterness and acid in both. But combine it with fat and throw in the right wine, and you have the hottest threesome in the land. Channelling umami's savoury, salty profile when choosing a bottle is a pro-move, particularly given the inbuilt salinity of many natural wines. Choose a non-aromatic variety with some extra structure via skin contact, sit back, and bliss out.

Try: Sticky miso pork or mushrooms and Nando Rebula (Ribolla Gialla) from Collio in Slovenia.

5. Sugar
There's a philosophy in the wine world that most wine goes with most food. There's also the concept that there is one titanic exception to this notion: *sugar*. This is how the theory goes: add any dry wine to food that contains even a hint of sweetness and observe how every last iota of deliciousness departs from your palate, leaving a trail of bitterness and despair in its wake. While this may be truer for conventional wines, natural wines tend to love a dare. Salinity and acidity in wine highlight any savoury notes in a dessert, while concurrently drawing out sweeter elements.

Try: Strawberry savarin with Crème Patissière and L'Archetipo Susumante Pét-nat from Puglia in Italy.

How to serve natural wine

A good chunk of the pompous reputation that follows wine has to be wrapped around the issue of how best to serve it. It can be a minefield. Which glassware? What are all the correct temperatures for different styles again? I am a charlatan if I buy a decanter and an even bigger one if I decant the wrong wine? What is a Coravin, and do I even need one? Serving wine can also be a subject of taste. Good sparkling wine tastes best when served from a wine glass, but I'm not one to get in the way of my fellow wine-drinker's desire for a flute or, heaven forbid, a coupette (although, confession: I stand by the philosophy that there is a time and place for a coupette). Some people swear wines taste better in certain glassware or even served via fish carafe, as somewhat inexplicably became the standard at a wine bar I used to run in Copenhagen.

When I first started working with natural wine, I loved the freedom of it. It was a style of wine for everyone, irrespective of your wine-drinking background, or if you could roll off a list of Burgundy's Grand Crus. With the growing popularity of natural wine came a sense of wine service dropping its shoulders a bit and the ability to ease away from excessive pageantry and have some actual fun.

Guarantee maximum deliciousness when drinking natural wine...

When all is said and done, wine should be served however you, the drinker, wants to do it. Mix it up and try new ways of serving wine, or if all else fails try my go-to hacks.

1. Know your environment

Are you hosting a party and planning to pour easy-going natural wines? If so, it's worth stocking up on smaller tasting wine glasses. You won't be able to detect all the aromas or witness the wine evolve in the glass, but that's not the point of this type of wine service. Your main priority is to create a relaxed environment for your fellow wine-drinkers to unwind in. Shatterproof govinos also work well if you are out and about, and they also allow you to get a real feel of a wine due to their shape. For all other occasions, a standard white wine glass should work well and allow you to capture the whole experience of your natural wine. Jancis Robinson glasses are my go-to for special natural wines that deserve a worthy platform.

2. Get a decanter and learn when to use it

I absolutely love decanting natural wine. It's my biggest power move when I'm in service and entertaining friends at home. With natural wines, white and skin-contact wines often benefit the most from air and movement to unravel their aromatics, but reds can be decanted, too. The main trick is to smell and taste the wine first: if it is a young wine and you'd like to see if it could become fruitier or more textural, pour it into a decanter. If your wine is reductive (smells like a freshly struck match), decant it vigorously. Don't be afraid to get some real air running through it. Keep the wine moving in the decanter; that aroma will start lifting off after a few minutes. If there is sediment in the bottle, it's worth decanting slowly with the bottle at a ninety-degree angle and the decanter or carafe at forty-five to keep the sediment from pouring out. Or, if you enjoy the textural offering of sediment, you can decant with a bit more gusto and create a snow-globe effect in the decanter.

3. Make sure the temperature is right
Temperature is everything when it comes to getting the best out of natural wine (and all wine, frankly). There is little nuance between the ideal service temperature for natural wines and their conventional counterparts. Still, it's worth remembering that natural wines often have more textural detail, and getting the temperature right when serving pays off. Let's start with fizz. If your pét-nat or other sparkling is sealed with a crown cap (aka a beer seal), ensure the fizz is as cold as possible before opening it slowly and carefully. The wine could have low or high pressure levels, so it's worth cooling it right down before opening it to ensure all the wine stays in the bottle once it's opened. Fridge temperature (6–9°C/43–48°F) is ideal. Richer styles of sparkling wine like crémant, Cava, or Champagnes can be served a little bit warmer than fridge temperature to highlight their breadth, creaminess, or any oxidative notes derived from the winemaking process.

Light, aromatic whites should be served just above fridge temperature. Skin-contact wines and full-bodied whites can be served a little warmer, so take them out of the fridge twenty minutes or so before you want to drink them so that they can achieve their textural potential. Light natural reds should be chilled, too, and will benefit from the narrowed focus provided to them by the temperature reduction. Putting these wines in the fridge twenty to thirty minutes before you want to drink them will do them a world of good. Heavier reds, if you buy them at room temperature, i.e. off a wine shop shelf, will also benefit from a slight chilling. Today's average room temperature hovers around 22°C (72°F), making any wine taste hot and bothered. Just put the wine in the fridge for fifteen minutes to get it back into balance before serving.

4. Other factors to consider
Like all wine, natural wine can be affected by irregularities or quirks. A wine that starts off reductive when opened can usually be remedied by a keen decant and/or lots of glass swirling. A corked wine (the aroma or taste of rotting wood or wet cardboard) will only worsen once it is opened, so it's worth moving it to the side and returning it to the shop. The same applies to mousiness (the taste of iodine, severely out-of-date popcorn or charmingly 'licking a mouse' – see glossary). Once a bottle reveals itself as mousy, it is likely to descend quickly, so it's best to bench it permanently. (If you are one of the lucky ones whose tongue pH can't detect mousiness, well, lucky you, the bottle is yours.)

5. Wine gadgets (aka the Coravin)
There are different views on how much impact pouring a wine through a Coravin makes on the wine's flavour. In restaurant or wine-bar service, using a Coravin allows us to open a wide selection of wines to pour by the glass, enabling us to find the right wine for everyone. Detractors say that wine poured by Coravin takes longer to open up in the glass, but, I find natural wines – particularly reds – have a habit of finding themselves much quicker so pouring via Coravin evens out the process. The obvious drawback to using a Coravin is the cost. And also the fact that you will definitely finish the bottle anyway because your wine is so moreish – and besides, you read the previous chapter and chose it like a pro.

HOW TO SERVE NATURAL WINE

RECIPES AND WINE PAIRINGS

Getting your head around what to cook with your wine – yes, that way round, please – can seem a daunting task, but the truth is, once you get started, learnings flow pretty naturally from there.

I've been lucky enough to work and make friends with the brilliant chefs whose recipes from around the world are found on the following pages.

RECIPES AND WINE PAIRINGS

RICE PAPER, APPLE & TAMARIND SALAD

Anaïs Ca Dao van Manen (Vietnam)

Born in Paris and raised in Vietnam, Anaïs Ca Dao van Manen is an unstoppable force of a cook. Having worked around the world in some of the globe's most riveting restaurants from London to Bogotá, she recently embarked on a journey of self-discovery in Vietnam and is currently writing her first cookbook dedicated to the country's often unsung cuisine.

Inspired by Vietnamese bánh tráng trộn, this dish is extremely versatile and fun to eat, a rice paper salad that is a great snack on its own, or as a side dish for those who love the chewy texture of rice or tapioca noodles. The dressing is sweet and sour, that comes from the tamarind paste. The latter differs depending on the brand, so feel free to adjust the levels of sweetness or tanginess depending on your personal liking. The idea here is to wilt your rice paper with the dressing, to soften it into chewy noodly bits. You can pimp this up with nuts, fried garlic, beef jerky, boiled quail eggs, shredded mango.

Serves 2

Spring onion relish
25g (3–4) spring onions, finely chopped
0.75g (⅛ tsp) fine salt
30ml (2 tbsp) neutral oil

Tamarind dressing
30ml (2 tbsp) tamarind paste
15ml (1 tbsp) light soy sauce
22.5ml maple syrup
1 long red chilli, deseeded and finely diced
1.5g (¼ tsp) salt

Salad
100g Granny Smith apple, thinly sliced
10g hot mint (also known as Vietnamese coriander/ cilantro, *rau răm*, or laksa leaf)
10g toasted peanuts, chopped
35g rice paper
15g crispy fried shallots

For the spring onion relish, mix the the spring onions with the salt in a non-reactive, heatproof bowl.

In a small saucepan, heat the oil gently until it reaches 180°C (350°F). Pour the oil over the spring onions and allow to cool.

Once cool, add all the tamarind dressing ingredients into the spring onion relish. This will become your final dressing.

Adjust the sweetness or tanginess to your liking with the maple syrup or soy sauce.

In a large mixing bowl, add the apple, hot mint and toasted peanuts. Cut the rice paper into strips and add to the bowl.

Dress with three-quarters of the final dressing and mix everything well with your hands, until the rice paper has softened. Pull apart any clumps of rice paper.

Put everything on a serving plate and drizzle over the remaining dressing.

Garnish with the fried shallots and serve immediately.

Pairing: Uivo Pét-Nat Branco (Folias de Baco – Douro, Portugal)
A lot of Vietnamese dishes beg for a side of bubbles in my experience, and none so more than this. Undergoing just the one fermentation, this pét-nat is outrageously restorative and refreshing, and teases out the full potential of the sweet-and-sour tamarind paste.

OX TONGUE SUYA WITH SMOKED BONE MARROW & RAMSON CAPERS

Ayo Adeyemi (Akoko, London)

Ayo is head chef at the celebrated West African restaurant Akoko in London's Fitzrovia. His detailed and flavoursome cooking has tempted me back many a time, and I have loved getting to know so many new flavours and spices over my visits.

A popular dish across West Africa, Suya is a traditional, smoked, spiced-meat skewer which originates in Hausa Land, Northern Nigeria. The key ingredient to suya spice is Kuli Kuli – a Nigerian peanut biscuit snack. Keep in mind that the ramson capers need 5 weeks to prepare for this dish, but they're well worth it!

Serves 6–8

Ox tongue
2 whole ox tongues
500ml (2 cups) 10% salt brine
10g thyme sprigs
1 whole garlic bulb, crushed
6 black peppercorns

Suya spice mix
200g peanuts (dry, unsalted)
   or store-bought Kuli Kuli
5g (1¾ tsp) ground ginger
2g (1¼ tsp) garlic powder
5g (2½ tsp) chilli powder
2g black peppercorns, ground
5g (¾ tsp) fine salt

Suya spice glaze
25g suya spice mix (above)
100ml water
25ml grapeseed oil
25g (3½ tsp) clear honey
100ml chicken stock
2 tsp chilli paste

Bone-marrow sabayon
70g (⅓ cup) butter
70g smoked bone marrow
   (or beef fat)
3g (⅔ tsp) sea salt
20ml Champagne vinegar
20ml lemon juice
80g egg yolk
60ml (¼ cup) water

Ramson (wild garlic) capers
500g ramson buds
75g (¼ cup) fine salt
200ml (⁴⁄₅ cup) white wine
vinegar

75ml (5 tbsp) water
75g (⅓ cup) sugar

OR use regular jarred capers

Ox tongue
Trim the sinew and excess fat from the ox tongues and combine with the rest of the ingredients in a large non-reactive bowl to brine overnight in the fridge.

Braise the ox tongues in a bain-marie for 20 hours until tender but still holding their form. Alternatively, you can pressure cook the ox tongue in a salted stock (no more than 1% salt solution) with aromatic herbs for around 45 minutes–1 hour.

Once cooked, drain and set aside to cool before peeling off the tough outer skin. Then press the ox tongues between two trays topped with a heavy weight and leave to chill in the fridge overnight.

Suya spice mix
Toast the peanuts on a baking tray in a preheated oven at 170°C/325°F/Gas Mark 3 for 10–15 minutes until golden brown. Set aside and allow to cool.

Blitz with the rest of the suya spice ingredients in a food processor or blender, into a fine crumb. (You only need 25g for this recipe but can store the rest to use another time.)

Suya spice glaze
Combine all the ingredients in a small saucepan and cook on a very low heat, for around 15 minutes, stirring continuously until it is reduced to a sticky glaze.

Bone-marrow sabayon
Combine all the sabayon ingredients in a medium pan and cook over a medium heat for 30 minutes, stirring occasionally. Then remove from the heat and blend with a stick blender until emulsified.

Continues overleaf ⟶

Charge in a siphon and store in a bain-marie at 65°C (149°F). Alternatively, whisk the egg yolks with the water, lemon juice, vinegar over a bain-marie to make a thick sabayon before whisking in the melted butter and beef fat (to essentially make a Béarnaise sauce), then serve immediately or keep warm in a bain-marie until ready to serve.

Ramson capers
Wash the ramson buds, then mix with the salt and store in the fridge, in a non-reactive sealed container, for 1 month.

When ready to use, rinse the salt from the ramson buds. Bring the vinegar, water, salt and sugar to the boil in a large pan then remove from the heat immediately and allow to cool. Add the mixture to the ramson buds and store in the fridge for at least a week before using.

If using regular jarred capers, fry them in vegetable oil at 200°C (390°F) for 10–15 seconds, until they become crispy. This adds texture and removes some of the saltiness.

To serve
Slice the ox tongues on a meat slicer or by hand at around 5mm thickness (around 10 slices per serving).

Pierce and arrange the slices neatly in layers onto one metal skewer per person. Brush the suya-spice glaze onto the meat and grill over a hot barbeque (or on a griddle pan on a high heat) for 1–2 minutes on each side until caramelized, adding more glaze as you go.

Pipe the bone-marrow sabayon onto each serving plate and gently place the grilled ox-tongue skewers to the side. Finish with an extra sprinkle of suya spice and a spoonful of ramson capers with a little of the pickling liquor.

Pairing: Pocco Rosso Syrah (Tom Shobbrook – Eden Valley, Australia)
This is a multi-dimensional pairing. This Syrah's own complex spice levels ramp up the heat in the suya, while the pure juiciness of the wine creates a wildly playful yet thoughtful fusion of spice, savoury, and sweet.

BURNT AUBERGINE WITH TAHINI & POMEGRANATE

Layo and Zoë Paskin (The Palomar, London)

Ten years ago my beloved bosses Zoë and Layo Paskin said goodbye to their iconic nightclub, The End, and put everything they had into creating The Palomar, a small restaurant on the corner of London's Chinatown, focused on modern Levantine cooking. The restaurant was an instant smash-hit and you'd be hard-pressed to find a foodie who doesn't adore it and visit whenever they are in the neighbourhood. This is one of their recipes from the early days, written for their 2016 eponymous recipe book *The Palomar Cookbook*.

You can think of this as a deconstructed baba ganoush. To get the maximum flavour from the aubergines, it's best to char them over an open flame on the hob or on a charcoal barbeque.

Serves 4–6

White tahini sauce
(Makes 250ml)
125ml (½ cup) tahini paste
100–125ml (approx. ½ cup)
    ice-cold water
juice of ½ a lemon
salt, to taste

Burnt aubergine
2 aubergines
salt and pepper, to taste
juice of half a lemon
60ml (4 tbsp) extra virgin
    olive oil, plus extra drizzle
    to garnish

To serve
60ml (4 tbsp) white tahini
    sauce (see left)
4 tbsp pomegranate seeds
handful of chopped
    fresh coriander

Continues overleaf ⟶

White tahini sauce

For a good tahini sauce, you need to start with a good tahini paste. Personally, I like Lebanese tahini, as it's rich and natural – the brand I use in the restaurant is Al Nakhil. Some like their tahini sauce with garlic, which I find overpowering; I like to really taste the sesame when I eat it.

Tahini is really the master paste, as you can put it on almost anything and it will make it taste better. But my favourite tahini marriage is with pitta or other bread. Any time of day or night is a good time to mop up some tahini with pitta; so simple but so tasty.

Before you start to make your sauce, it's important to point out that every tahini paste is a bit different, so the volume of water needed will change from brand to brand. The good news is that, if you add the water slowly, you'll be able to judge when you've hit the right texture. And what is the right texture, you ask? It all depends how you like it! I like it to be somewhere in the middle so that when you dip a spoon and lift it, the tahini oozes down slowly. There's no right or wrong – some like it very runny, some like it thick and dense – I like it in the middle!

Spoon the tahini paste into a bowl, add the water gradually and beat constantly with a whisk. At first the tahini will become denser (don't panic!) and then it will start to loosen up. Stop when you hit the texture you like.

Add the lemon juice and salt to taste.

You can keep the sauce refrigerated, tightly covered with cling film, for up to 2 days (it goes a bit thicker in the fridge).

Burnt aubergine

Prick the aubergines in several places with the tip of a sharp knife so that they won't explode in your face and make a mess in the kitchen.

Char the aubergines on all sides over an open flame on the hob or hot charcoal on a barbeque, turning every 5–6 minutes, until the skin hardens up and gets a bit crispy.

There is a third option: set your grill to the highest setting and roast the aubergines in the closest position to the heat source, turning in the same way.

Leave the aubergines until cool enough to handle, then peel.

You can keep the aubergines in an airtight container in the fridge for 2–3 days, and, when you want to serve, simply heat them up and add your garnishes.

To serve

Arrange the whole burnt, peeled aubergines on a serving plate, then season to taste with salt and pepper.

Dress with the lemon juice and olive oil. Drizzle the white tahini sauce on top, sprinkle with the pomegranate seeds and the chopped coriander and drizzle with a little more olive oil.

Pairing: Rosé Supernova (Schödl – Wienviertel, Austria)
This rosé has to be one of the most happiness-inducing wines on the planet. It gives 'ice-cold watermelon on a hot day' and contented summer stickiness alongside a depth of flavour and texture not usually associated with rosé – and absolutely custom-made for pomegranate.

RAZOR CLAMS & OLD WINCHESTER

Holly and Brad Carter (Carters of Moseley, Birmingham)

Carters of Moseley is my favourite restaurant in the UK. Chef Brad Carter and his wife Holly offer a multi-course tasting menu, with particular attention to the best produce, foraged flora and wild fauna indigenous to the UK. Their cooking style uses ancestral techniques like fire and fermentation blended with a modern spirit of creative culture and deep insight into each ingredient's history. And let's not forget the wine: Holly's list is a thoughtful curation of some of the world's best naturals; her pairing menu is one of my all-time favourites.

This is my take on 'cacio e pepe' and is my favourite dish both to cook and eat. I've reworked it with alternative ingredients as I only use UK produce in the restaurant. Instead of pasta, I use razor clams and cut them to resemble penne – there's a natural hole running through the middle. I use Old Winchester cheese – the closest thing we have to Parmesan in the UK – it's aged at Lyburn Dairy in Wiltshire for twenty-six months just for our dish. As black pepper doesn't grow here because of our climate, I use a seaweed called pepper dulse. It gets its name from its slight spice (reminiscent of black pepper), and is collected by our foragers from the coast. I dry out the fronds, grind in a pepper grinder and then make an oil out of the stems.

Serves 2

50g (¼ cup) dried white beans (such as coco or cannellini), soaked overnight
½ carrot, peeled, halved lengthways
½ leek, trimmed, halved lengthways
½ onion, peeled, halved
½ celery stick

1 garlic clove
1 sprig thyme
5g (¾ tsp) salt
265g Old Winchester cheese, grated
8 live fresh razor clams, washed under running water to remove any grit (discard any clams that don't close tightly when tapped)

pinch of dried pepper dulse
   or black pepper, to serve
drizzle of pepper dulse oil or
   olive oil, to serve

Drain the beans, put in a large saucepan and add the vegetables. Cover with 2 litres (8 cups) of water. Bring to the boil and simmer for 40 minutes, until the beans are tender.

Add the garlic, thyme and half a teaspoon of salt, then pour the mixture onto a deep baking tray to stop the cooking process. Leave to cool. Once cool, strain the stock into a clean measuring jug, discarding the vegetables. Put the beans into a clean bowl and pour over enough of the stock to cover.

Pour 900ml (3½ cups) of the stock into a pan and bring to the boil. Add the cheese and the remaining salt. Remove from the heat and blend with a hand-held blender. Allow to cool, then put in the fridge overnight.

The following day, strain the liquid through a fine sieve into a clean pan and reheat gently in a large pan.

Open the razor clams by pulling the shells apart, then cut the meat away from the shells. Cut the top white meat on the angle into two pieces to represent penne pasta.

When the broth has reached a simmer, put the clams into the cheese broth and turn off the heat. Leave to stand for 1 minute. To serve, spoon the broth into bowls, season with the dried pepper dulse, and drizzle over the pepper dulse oil.

Pairing: Feel Good (Frédéric Cossard – Burgundy, France)
From a parcel planted with fifty-year-old vines, this Savagnin is vinified in the Burgundian (*ouillé*) style and aged in concrete eggs for a year. Like many natural whites, it's totally electric and brings a similar vibrancy to the dish, singling out the nuttiness of the Old Winchester and highlighting the spice from the pepper dulse.

SINGAPORE LAKSA

Elizabeth Haigh (Mei Mei, London)

Owner of the extoled Singaporean spot, Mei Mei, at the heart
of London's Borough Market, Liz Haigh makes food that makes
people happy. We once hosted a festive pop-up together
showcasing her Michelin-starred cooking and my favourite
suitcase-import natural wines, and it was nothing short of joyous.

This recipe is a taste of home for me. Laksa is so popular
back home in Singapore, but did you know there are around
nine different types of laksa? This particular version is
my favourite, developed by my mother who insists that
you should always start with a really good broth/stock and
plenty of aromatic herbs/spices to make a laksa worthy of
Singapore's title. If you aren't making your own fishcakes,
don't worry, go to any South-East Asian supermarket and
they will have packets of fresh or frozen variety.

Serves 4

Spice paste
2cm piece galangal
5 candlenuts (or macadamia
  nuts)
125g shallots, peeled, sliced
½ tsp turmeric powder
6–8 medium red chillies,
  deseeded
15g belachan, toasted
  (fermented shrimp paste)
30g dried shrimps, soaked in
  boiling water for 20 minutes,
  drained and patted dry

Laksa
400g laksa noodles (or dry
  rice vermicelli)
30ml (2 tbsp) cooking oil
1 stick lemongrass, crushed
15g (1 tbsp) ground coriander

1 litre (4 cups) good-quality
  chicken or prawn stock
400ml can coconut milk
2 tsp salt
15g (1 tbsp) sugar
300g raw large prawns, head
  on, shell removed and
  deveined
1–2 fried Chinese fishcakes,
  sliced 0.5cm thick (see
  below)
150g beansprouts, blanched
  in boiling water for 30
  seconds and drained
1 cucumber, peeled and cut thin
  on a spiraliser or into strips
small bunch of laksa leaves,
  shredded (aka Vietnamese
  mint/coriander; or use
  coriander leaves)

Spice paste
Whizz the spice paste ingredients in a blender until smooth, adding 30–45ml (2–3 tbsp) of coconut milk to help it blend smoothly. Keep to one side.

Laksa
Soak the laksa noodles/rice vermicelli in warm water for 30 minutes, then drain and keep to one side. Rinse under cold water to prevent the noodles from sticking.

Heat the oil in a large saucepan over a medium heat and stir in the spice paste for 2–3 minutes or until fragrant. Add the lemongrass and cook over a low heat for 10–15 minutes, stirring often to stop the paste sticking to the bottom of the pan. Add a splash of water occasionally to stop it burning. Stir in the ground coriander and cook for 5 minutes more (adding more water as needed).

Next pour in the chicken or prawn stock and simmer for around 5 minutes. Add the coconut milk and stir until it boils, lower the heat and simmer for another 10–15 minutes to give a rich soup. Season with salt and add a small pinch of sugar to give it a rounder flavour.

Heat a large pan of water to boiling point and add the softened laksa noodles/rice vermicelli to blanch for 1 second. It is important to make sure not to overcook them. If using thicker noodles for laksa, boil for longer until they are cooked through.

To serve
Divide the prawns and all the remaining ingredients, except the laksa leaves, between four bowls. Pour the soup over the top of each and scatter with a pinch of laksa leaves.

Pairing: Little Bastard (Staffelter Hof – Mosel, Germany)
I paired this over a summer evening at Mei Mei in Borough Market with this white from Jan Klein of Staffelter Hoff in the Mosel and have thought of it often over the years. The spiciness of the laksa is simultaneously boosted and abated by the pinch of maceration and creamy depth of this Riesling blend.

MUSHROOM DUMPLINGS & DASHI

Luke Selby (Evelyn's Table, London)

In 2018, chef Luke Selby and his brothers Nat and Theo started cooking in the former keg rooms of The Blue Posts pub in London's Soho. The twelve-seater counter-dining restaurant was called Evelyn's Table, and in the years since has become one of the most coveted dinner spots in the city, picking up its first Michelin star in 2022. I was lucky enough to build the wine program with Luke and our inimitable restaurant manager Aidan Monk.

An autumnal dish I created for Honey during my time at Evelyn's Table in London. The broth – deep with umami flavour – is comforting and packed with savoury deliciousness, perfect and simple to cook at home.

Serves 4

Mushroom dashi
1kg button mushrooms, sliced
pinch of salt
30ml (2 tbsp) dark soy sauce
500ml (2 cups) water
20g kombu (kelp)
15g katsuobushi flakes
   (dried tuna)

Gyozas
250g mushrooms, leftover
   from the dashi (see above)
250g button mushrooms,
   diced
10g butter
1 clove garlic, pureed
pinch of salt
1 packet gyoza (dumpling)
   skins

20ml (1⅓ tbsp) sesame oil
20ml (1⅓ tbsp) water
1 bunch of spring onions,
   thinly sliced, to serve

Pickled shimeji mushrooms
50g shimeji mushrooms
50ml (3⅓ tbsp) white wine
   vinegar
20ml (1⅓ tbsp) water
pinch of salt
pinch of sugar

Mushroom dashi

Place the mushrooms, salt, soy, water and kombu in a large, flat-bottom saucepan with a tight-fitting lid and bring to a boil. Simmer on the lowest heat for 20 minutes and pass through a sieve keeping the liquid. Set the mushrooms aside for the gyoza filling (see below).

Add the katsuobushi flakes into the mushroom liquid and leave to infuse for 10 minutes, then pass through a fine sieve, keeping the liquid.

Gyozas and pickled shimeji mushrooms

Blend the leftover dashi mushrooms in a blender into a smooth purée. In a medium saucepan over a medium heat, cook the button mushrooms in the butter with the garlic and salt, then mix together with the blended mushrooms, transfer to a bowl, and chill in the fridge. When ready to cook, weigh into 15g portions and wrap into the gyoza skins.

Meanwhile, make the pickled shimeji mushrooms. Add all the ingredients to a pan and bring to a boil, then take off the heat to cool and leave to infuse.

To cook the gyozas, heat the sesame oil in a large lidded pan. Fry on one side only until golden, then add the water, and quickly place the lid on top and steam for 4 minutes. Remove the lid and continue to cook for a further 2 minutes until the water has evaporated and the gyozas are cooked.

Meanwhile, bring the mushroom dashi to a boil, then serve in ramen bowls with the gyozas. Garnish with the pickled shimeji mushrooms and sliced spring onion.

Pairing: Conasbrancas (Fedellos – Galicia, Spain)
This Albariño-based field blend is jaw-droppingly good. It delivers a high-impact dose of acidity, along with a broad minerality and saltiness that fuses with the umami of the mushrooms and soy, revealing a perfect sweetness in the dashi.

FROM OBAN (TO MARSEILLE), WITH LOVE

Megan Moore (Marseille)

Megan Moore is one of those chefs who seem to be everywhere at once. Born in Glasgow, she moved to London and worked for iconic restaurants such as F.K.A.B.A.M (formerly known as Black Axe Mangal) and KOL before travelling the world and (semi) settling in Marseille. These days, she goes wherever the pop-ups take her, learning and creating along the way. This dish expresses her love of both her Scottish hometown of Oban and her new base in the South of France.

A place I love to visit whenever I go home is the Oban Seafood Hut (the green shack). Fresh crab sandwiches, lobster, oysters, and their famous Lambrini mussels. Super-simple pan-fried soft and sweet onions, mussels and Lambrini to finish, a very lovable nostalgic dish. Since living in Marseille, my right of passage is becoming a pastis drinker. Not to everyone's taste, the anise-y-liquorice flavour put me off at first, but slowly, with the right amount of water, I grew to love it waking me up on a sweaty Marseille afternoon. Here enters, Chez Gilda. A hole-in-the-wall shellfish place in the city, pastis prawns, local octopus and mangetout, fried whitebait. I eat here about twice a week when they are open. The pastis prawns with a touch of harissa transported me home to the Lambrini mussels with a drizzle of Tabasco. This recipe is the love child of these two.

Serves 2

⅓ of a cucumber, peeled and halved lengthways
½ a green chilli, deseeded
good pinch of salt
small pinch of sugar
30ml (2 tbsp) rice or apple cider vinegar

olive oil
⅓ a leek, chopped in thinnish rounds
4–6 king/tiger prawns, head on, shell removed and deveined

100g clams or mussels,
cleaned
1 garlic clove
30ml (2 tbsp) pastis
30ml (2 tbsp) white or
orange wine

1 bunch of chives, chopped
finely
squeeze of lemon juice
Tabasco, optional

Place the blade of a large knife flat on the cucumber and smash down lightly with your other hand. Chop up the length of the cucumber into chunks, then place it in a bowl with the chilli. Add the salt, sugar, and vinegar, mix together and put in the fridge.

Take a large frying pan, set on a medium heat, add the olive oil and caramelize the leeks with a pinch of salt. Once they are soft, turn up to a high heat.

Push the leeks to the side, then add the prawns and let them fry for a short time before adding the clams or mussels. Keep on a high heat and let some of the water evaporate before adding the garlic and then pastis and wine; the wine softens and stretches the pastis.

Cover with a lid for 20–30 seconds to steam the clams or mussels until they open. Take off the lid and turn down the heat – there should not be too much liquid. If it's a little thin you can add in a small chunk of butter, which will also make it a little more rich and glossy if you prefer a creamy style. Remove from the heat and add the chopped chives and lemon juice. Toss together.

Take the cucumber and chilli mix from the fridge and remove from the bowl to leave behind any liquid. Add to the pan, toss quickly and check the seasoning. Add Tabasco to taste, if you wish. Serve immediately, in bowls, before the cucumber heats up.

Pairing: Lechkhumi Tsolikouri (Igavi Wines – Imereti, Georgia)
Wild and free, this wine seems to perfectly capture the taste of sea air, despite hailing from Georgia's land-locked Imereti wine region. It has those vibratory qualities that natural wine drinkers often talk about, as well as a crunchy hint of herbs and citrus.

OSSOBUCO ALLA MILANESE

Mitshel Ibrahim (Ombra and Forno, London)

Mitshel Ibrahim is head chef and partner of East London's darling Italian eateries Ombra and Forno. Ombra is a Venetian colloquialism for 'little tumbler'. 'When you want to have a little wine safari around the neighbourhood, having a glass here and a glass there, you'll say, "Let's go for an Ombra!",' Mitshel tells me. He loves wine, and I've had my fair share of life-affirming natural wines within a few strides of his kitchen while dining at Ombra over the years.

Ossobuco is one of the most famous Milanese dishes. Seeing as I was born in Milan, I have a personal attachment to the dish, which naturally holds some feelings of nostalgia and pride. It's a wintery dish that uses a great piece of meat and takes a bit of work to make. This is why as a family we used to cook and eat it on a Sunday. Flip side, it's a one-pot dish, so once you've cooked it a few times, you can just let it be while you get on chatting to friends and pouring a glass of wine.

Serves 2 (hungry people)

Ossobuco
2 veal beef shins (3–4cm thick, cut through the bone)
30g (2 tbsp) buckwheat flour
50g (3⅓ tbsp) unsalted butter
1 red onion, chopped
a glass of dry white wine, such as Verdicchio
500ml (2 cups) chicken or veal stock
a few sprigs of thyme
salt and pepper, to season

Gremolata
olive oil
3 garlic cloves, grated
zest of 2 unwaxed organic lemons
a small bunch of flat-leaf parsley, roughly chopped

Pairing: due M (Le Coste – Lazio, Italy)
Intense, heady, and wildly perfumed, this skin-contact Moscato Giallo and a local variety of Moscato tightens and brightens the ossobuco, while allowing it to retain its wintery, warming comfort.

Dust the veal shins in buckwheat flour, making sure to cover all of the meat. Add some olive oil to a flameproof casserole dish over a medium–high heat. *Note: The dish should be wide enough to fit the meat in, but not so wide that the stock will be too shallow once added – the width of the dish is key.*

Add the butter to the casserole dish and colour the meat (around 3–4 minutes on each side) to make sure each side has browned. Remove the meat and set aside. Add the onion to the pan and fry gently until soft. Then add the wine and reduce the liquid down a little. Once the onion has softened, put the meat back into the casserole dish, sitting on top of the onion. Pour the stock over so that it comes up to three-quarters of the height of the meat and bring to the boil.

Then reduce to a low heat, cover the dish with a lid and bring to a simmer. Add the thyme and season to taste, then leave the lid slightly ajar so that steam can escape and help the sauce reduce down. The buckwheat flour will help thicken the sauce and give it a nice nutty, biscuity flavour. Set a timer for 30 minutes and then turn the meat over for a further 10–30 minutes depending on the size of the cut. You want the meat to gently cook through so it does not dry out; this is the key to keeping it tender.

While the meat is cooking, make the gremolata. In a small bowl, mix the garlic, lemon, and parsley, then add a touch of olive oil to bring the three ingredients together. Gently mix.

Once the meat is cooked, carefully remove it from the casserole dish and set aside. Strain the cooking liquid into a heatproof bowl or jug to remove any larger ingredients and then pour the sauce back into the casserole dish over a medium–high heat to reduce it to a nice jus consistency.

To serve, spoon the jus over the meat and add the gremolata over the top – it will lift the flavours and add a citrusy zest to balance the meat. Traditionally ossobuco is served with a saffron risotto, or try with a crisp, fresh salad to keep it light.

MEXICAN CORN WITH CHILLI MAYONNAISE & COMTÉ

Nick Fitzgerald (Tacos Padre, London)

I met Nick at one of his iconic summer BBQs sometime around the mid 2010s. I was struck by his talents of throwing a great house party, grilling like a pro, and knowing a great deal about good wine. Needless to say, we've been good friends ever since. When he's not scouring Mexico for inspiration, the former Pujol and Clove Club chef can be found at his beloved Taco stand, Tacos Padre, in London's Borough Market.

Believe it or not, I was once a cheesemonger. I was forever astonished at how mad people could be for cheese; at times I felt as though I knew what a drug dealer must feel like. Comté was always the go-to, especially the reserve. The silky nature of the cheese sliced with a tasting spatula still brings back great memories. Everyone was a fan, so it was an easy sell. British corn is some of the best I've ever had. I believe it's some of the best in the world. We get ours from Maldon in Essex and when it arrives, we steam it first then grill it hard. The combination of pasilla and chipotle chillies is a good substitute for one of the most incredible chillies in Mexico – Pasilla Mixe. Mixe is a pre-Hispanic culture and region which grows and smokes this chilli. This combination is a clever hack that we use if we don't have Pasilla Mixe.

Serves 6 (as a side dish)

10g chipotle chilli
30g pasilla chilli
3 egg yolks
5g salt
juice of 2 limes

500ml (2 cups) neutral oil,
    such as rapeseed
3 ears of corn, with husk
any hard Alpine cheese,
    such as Comté or Parmesan
lime wedges, to garnish

Destem the chillies and add to a blender. Blend until smooth – around 2 minutes should do it. Strain the blended chillies through a fine strainer to create a purée.

To make the chilli mayonnaise, thoroughly clean the blender. This will ensure you are able to make a stable emulsion. Add to the blender, the egg yolks, salt, chilli purée and lime juice. Blend for 30 seconds then slowly add the oil until the consistency becomes thick, glossy and smooth. Season with salt to taste.

Steam or boil the ears of corn (with the husk still on) for around 10 minutes until tender, then drain off any water and grill them over a very hot barbeque or grill to give them a good char.

Chop the corn in half and coat thoroughly in the spicy mayonnaise. Transfer to a serving dish and finely grate your chosen cheese over the top.

Serve with a chunk of lime on the side for extra vibes.

Pairing: Y'a Plus Qu'à (Kumpf & Meyer – Alsace, France)
The ideal wine for a dish that has sweet, salt, and acid in abundance. This Alsatian white, made of Auxerrois and Sylvaner, has everything: flowers, mineral, acidity, and fruit, plus a subtle savoury undertone that lifts every flavour it meets.

CONVINCING
A CRITIC

In 2017, I scored my first Head Sommelier role in London. I had just returned from a two-year stint in Copenhagen, and my head overflowed with dreams of bringing natural wine to every corner and crevice of my hometown. The restaurant was in London's 'white-collar' district, awash with skyscrapers and likely half of Mendoza's annual Malbec production lurking in cellars below the concrete kingdom. I was young, idealistic, and utterly ecstatic at being entrusted with a wine list. My goal was simple enough: give natural wine to those who are up for it and organic wine to everyone else. I divided the list into four categories: Tried & True, The Classics, A Touch Out of The Ordinary, and Wild Things. The first two consisted of varieties, regions, and flavours that most everyday wine drinkers could recognize. The wines were made organically or biodynamically with minimal intervention, but were fairly pedestrian in terms of flavour. A Touch Out of The Ordinary had slightly off-the-beaten-track wines, either from lesser-known regions or varieties, or slightly more left-field in taste. Wild Things had, of course, the naturals, made with as little intervention as possible and tasting as such – untamed, uninhibited, and a hell of a lot of fun. At the heart of it was the hope that guests would be able to order according to how adventurous they felt in the moment without fear of judgement or looking like a dolt in front of the group.

The restaurant opened as well as it could, and I was in my element, hurtling around the one-hundred-seat venue, popping corks with my sommelier co-pilot Ellen and doing our best not to upset any suits or boomers who really did just want a bottle of Malbec (to my memory, we did list one). Life was good, great even, until one Friday night, with the dining room in full swing, I saw a shape at the door. Not just any shape, *the* shape of *The Guardian* food critic Jay Rayner making his way into the restaurant. Anyone who has ever worked in a restaurant, or even watched the movie *Ratatouille*, understands the sheer terror that accompanies the sight of a food critic. A mere flick of the wrist over a keyboard can declare a future icon or condemn a restaurant to a terrible death, often in its first weeks and months of opening. With this critic, there was another pretty gargantuan problem. Jay Rayner *hated* natural wine. In fact, his loathing of it was so deeply entrenched that should a restaurant he visited feature natural wine, the entire subsequent column would be dedicated to ensuring the poor sommelier in question would rue the day they ever so much as looked at a grape.

My eyes locked with my fellow manager as we wordlessly hashed together a plan, while also taking a moment to concede this might be our last night on Earth. Table A (designated for the booking, which was unsurprisingly not in his real name) was quickly swapped with Table B (more spacious and with a better view of the kitchen). Waiter X (sweet but likely to pulverize under pressure) was swapped with Waiter Y (chatty and confident, also likely to have no awareness of our guest, which could only protect against pulverization). As I walked the twenty or so excruciating paces over to the table at which our guest and his own were now sitting, I considered ripping out the last two pages of the wine list, saving my career from certain peril, or repatriation to an island in the Pacific. I introduced myself, immediately unsure as to why I had given my name and not someone else's, and then explained the wine list before staggering into the chefs' walk-in fridge.

An order came through the bar docket printer: one bottle of organic producer Luneau-Papin, a Loire wine from A Touch Out of The Ordinary. The wine itself was simple and delicious, but its appeal positioning on this page was due to the inclusion of a rare grape variety named Folle Blanche. A nod was issued. I commissioned myself a moment of reprieve before returning to the bedlam of a pre-Covid Friday night in the city, unsure if I would live to somm another day.

Weeks passed. And then, one Sunday morning on an overnight stay at biodynamic wine-growers Ancre Hill in Wales, I awoke to a shriek from my best friend Kate next to me, her face lit up by her phone as she delivered my fate:

'Yes, it has a bunch of fearsome "naturals". But they are cordoned off on their own page under the heading "Wild Things". There are other pages called "Tried and True", "The Classics," and "A Touch Out of the Ordinary". It's a wine list with a map. If you want to experiment, you can. If you want to go vanilla, you can do that, too. Other restaurants should come and study the wine list to see how it's done.'

I looked downward at the phone, blinking my eyes in disbelief. I thought of all the brilliant natural wine lists scattered around the city and the sommeliers I had turned to for advice while writing my own. I thought of all the city's natural-wine detractors and the everyday wine-drinkers who might now be spurred to give it a chance and discover something new. Perhaps I would live to somm another day after all.

WHAT
HAPPENS
NOW?

It's not hard to see how wine has come to mean so much to so many people over such a long span of time on our small but pithy planet. For centuries, wine has been a symbol of humanity, of defiance and resilience, of creativity, of our ability to work with nature, a pledge for the future. Many wine-growers plant vineyards with the knowledge that they will be long gone by the time their vines will produce the wines they are truly capable of.

For those of us who live with the wine bug, it's never too far from our minds. We think of when and how to buy it, how best to store it, and how to bring it out when it might be showing its best (if you have the patience to wait, a rare occurrence in my house), how to serve it, what to serve it with, and who to serve it to. To say wine is an agricultural product would, of course, be true, but, in fact, it is so much more. Wine is a moment caught in time, never – before or since – able to be replicated in exactly the same way. Wine is a time capsule, a picture of a year, of a place, of those who grow the grapes and guide them into bottle. To echo the sentiments of my wine-grower friend Stephanie...

'Viticultural products can travel and tell their story all over the world. Tell the story of a piece of earth and a particular time.'

Natural wine, then, is all of the above but in raw, unedited format. Like the picture of the person you love first thing in the morning, full of sleep and slowness, versus the photoshoot picture, obscured by filters and practised pouts. I know which version I prefer.

I have always distanced myself from dogma, not as a reflection of my personal tenets, but more because I am, first and foremost, a server. My irrevocable MO is to look after people, make them feel at home, and find something tasty for them to eat and drink. Yes, I am fiercely protective of natural wine, but even more protective of my guests' experience. However, if I can persuade my guests to open their minds a little and try something new, then that's a bonus.

I'm not trying to win you over to natural wine with this book. There are plenty of people who have decided natural wine isn't for them, and that is very much okay. Natural wine still only accounts for one per cent of global wine production, so there's not that much of it to go around in the first place. And besides, not everyone wants to drink natural wine, and not all wine-growers can make natural wine. For a truly delicious natural wine to be made, the grapes must be harvested at the right time, under the right conditions, from practically perfect vineyards that have themselves equilibrium and can withstand the trials of the ever-changing climate, such as disease pressure and drought, along with minimal interference in the winery. It's also fair to say not every natural wine is good, but then again, not every conventional wine is good either; far, far from it.

And yet, there is something deeply romantic about natural wine. In a world of identikit international varieties, it is a revolt. It is a revolt against hi-tech, against the constant, crushing pressure to expand, scale up, save resources (whose?), or time (what would we really do with more time?). It's the refusal to accept the concept of growth as purely in quantitative terms rather than the growth of our thoughts, values, intellect, or integrity. To choose natural wine is to support artisans, many of whom have adopted a radically regenerative approach to safeguarding our rapidly depleting soils, which the UN have predicted will only be able to support life on Earth for another fifty to sixty years. Of course, at this point, wine will be the absolute lowest priority (well, for *most* of us) when it comes to deciding what and how we feed ourselves next. So, in truth, 'natural' is something we should all be moving towards in many senses.

And then there's the *taste* element, which many wine-lovers would argue is as important, if not more important, than the ethical framework in which wine, by its nature, sits.

While I don't totally agree, I do believe it's still important to have a nice time on this planet while we are here and drink some tasty things.

So, here's where the advice comes in. Try a few natural wines. Find one that you like and work out what you enjoy about it. Find a sommelier or retailer you trust and let them help you figure out other natural wines you might like, too. As I've mentioned already, wine is expensive. It is an investment and, as such, also a risk. A good sommelier or retailer who knows your palate will help mitigate that risk. Try, if you can, to step outside the boundaries we have set for our wine experiences and dare to derive enjoyment out of flavours that go beyond fruit, oak, and forest floor. Look for salt; look for savoury and intriguing qualities. Embrace wines that make you think, make you feel, make you question, make you wonder. If you don't like a particular wine, ask yourself why, and then feel free to move on. You've just made your sommelier's life a lot easier the next time around. If your wine tastes like wet cardboard, rotting wood, or balsamic vinegar, don't feel ashamed to question it; it's important to find wines you like, wines that have been made with care and kept in the right condition. Try to see wine as food, something that you put into your body to nourish you. Take a wine course, even a generic one. It will heighten your overall enjoyment of wine and is likely to make you realize how much you love natural wine compared to its generic and static counterparts.

For those of us who love wine, every cork popped brings with it the chance of a new discovery, a new taste, a smell, a new evocation. It is a special opportunity to taste a place, a person, and a moment in time. Natural wine brings with it the freedom of exploration without expectation, hierarchy, or pomp.

If you've read this book to this last line, then hoorah, you already know what to ask for when you're searching for your next bottle...

Natural wine, but please, no drama.

A year around the
world of natural wine

Whenever I ask myself whether natural wine is still confined to the fringes of wine culture, I seem to stumble on another event packed to the rafters of interesting and diverse producers pouring their wines in every type of spot: in fields, up mountains, in aviaries, historic marketplaces, warehouses, and old dockyards. Aaron Ayscough's substack 'Not Drinking Poison' has an almost all-encompassing list of seasonal events updated regularly, but here is my trip around the world in twelve of the best events.

January
Bottled Alive, Tabor, Czech Republic
@bottledalive

This intimate winemakers' symposium, organized by Thir Wine Bar owner Jan Čulík, is a love-in for some of Central and Eastern Europe's most pioneering and progressive winemakers. Now in its seventh year, all producers must adhere to the following criteria: the grapes must come from organic vineyards, be fermented with natural yeasts, only coarsely filtered (if at all), and contain 66.6mg/litre of total sulphites. Regular pourers include Slovakia's Slobodne, NABOSO, and Milan Nestarec; Austria's Claus Preisinger, Heinrich, and Michael Gindl; and Germany's Jas Swan. A small selection of French and Italian producers also have a habit of joining the party – likely as a welcome distraction away from Europe's coldest month.

Wine-growers to try: Slobodne and NABOSO (Bratislava, Slovakia), Milan Nestarec (Moravia, Czech Republic), Claus Preisinger, Heinrich, and Michael Gindl (Burgenland, Austria), and Jas Swan (Katla Wines, Mosel, Germany).

February
Salon St Jean, Angers, France
@degustationgrenierstjean

Possibly the world's best wine fair with the worst website, it is almost impossible to find any information on Salon St Jean until three days before the event. Nevertheless, every year, it shows up at the same time (the first weekend in February) and the same place (Place du Tertre Saint-Laurent) in the Loire Valley city of Angers. Swarming with members of the natural-wine posse Renaissance des Appellations, this would be practically a one-stop shop for Europe's natural winemakers if you didn't consider that the same weekend holds Les Pénitentes, Chai!, Salon des Vins Nat' et S.A.I.N.S, Salon de Rablay, Les Anonymes, and natural wine's answer to Coachella, La Dive Bouteille, held in Saumur's limestone caves, all within a short driving distance. In short, this is your sign to take a trip to the Loire Valley next February.

Wine-growers to try: Julien Guillot (Clos Des Vignes du Mayne, Burgundy, France), Domaine Mann (Alsace, France), Comte Abbatucci (Corsica, France), Frederico Orsi (Emilia-Romagna, Italy), Domaine de Beudon (Valais, Switzerland).

Salon O, Seoul, South Korea
@salono_naturalwine

Despite vowing to stay strictly to one event per month, an extra special mention should be directed to Salon O in Seoul, an event that has captured the hearts and palates of wine-lovers in South Korea and is frequented by some of the biggest names in the natural wine business.

Wine-growers to try: Aurélien & Charlotte Houillon (Rhône, France), Charles Dufour (Champagne, France) Lammidia (Abruzzo, Italy), Vinyes Tortuga (Catalunya, Spain).

March
Third Coast Soif, Chicago, US
@thirdcoastsoif

A Chicago fair celebrating minimal intervention wines, ciders, and beers grown and made naturally and poured for the people who thirst for them. Featuring on average seventy producers, pouring over 350 wines from North America and Europe.

Wine-growers to try: Hiyu Wine Farm and Ovum Wines (Oregon, US), Phelan Farm and Lo-Fi (California, US), Mersel Wine (Lebanon), Kamara (Thessaloniki, Greece), Arianna Occhipinti (Sicily, Italy), and Fruktstereo (Sweden).

April
The Real Wine Fair, London, UK
@realwinefair

A bi-annual celebration of the labour, craft, and skill of small, independent vine-growers. There are four simple objectives: to showcase some of the world's most talented artisan vignerons under one roof; to illustrate the existing diversity and personality of naturally made wines; to allow growers and customers to exchange information and ideas, and, of course, to have a bloody good knees up. Hosted by natural wine sweetheart distributors Les Caves de Pyrene (see page 58).

Wine-growers to try: Folias de Baco (Douro, Portugal), Jugo Vins (Mallorca, Spain), Charlie Herring (England, UK), Vino di Anna (Sicily, Italy) Domaine Mosse (Loire, France), Jauma (South Australia).

May
Zero Compromise, Tbilisi, Georgia
@naturalwineassociation

Held in a former silk factory, this is Georgia's biggest celebration of traditionally made natural wines from the artisans, helping to keep Georgian natural wine-growing alive. Created by celebrated vignerons John Wurdeman of Pheasant's Tears and John Okruashvili of Okro's Wines in association with the National Wine Agency of Georgia, this two-day celebration of the world's 'cradle of wine' is your sign to book a flight.

Wine-growers to try: Nikoladzeebis Marani and Archil Guniava (Imereti, Georgia), Iago Winery (Kartli, Georgia), Pheasant's Tears (Kakheti, Georgia).

June
Feira Naturebas, São Paulo, Brazil
@feiranaturebas

Now in its twelfth year, Feira Naturebas is the first and only wine fair in Brazil specializing in natural, organic, and biodynamic wines and ferments, little by little becoming a reference on the subject in Latin America. Mainly Brazilian producers with a scattering of artisans from elsewhere in South America, such as Uruguay, Chile, Argentina, and Bolivia, as well as a pinch of travel-hungry producers from further afield. Curated by Lis Cereja and Leo Reis, founders of fêted São Paulo wine bar and restaurant Enoteca Saint VinSaint.

Wine-growers to try: Vivente and Era dos Ventos (Brazil), Escala Humana Wines (Valle de Uco, Argentina).

July
H2O Vegetal, Catalunya, Spain

Birthed by Catalan vignerons Joan Ramon Escoda (see page 93), and Laureano Serres (of Mendall), this is an annual alfresco event that brings together the cream of the crop of Catalan natural wine-growers, plus a close-knit curation of vignerons who share the same zero-zero sensibilities. Named H2O Vegetal as a nod to natural wine's hydrating and rejuvenating properties! But do try and stay hydrated on real water, too.

Wine-growers to try: Escoda-Sanahuya, Mendall, Clos Lentiscus, Partida Creus (Catalunya, Spain), Microbio (Castilla y León, Spain).

August
Farmhouse Fest, Vancouver, Canada
@farmhousefest

A more recent addition to the global natural wine fair landscape is Farmhouse Fest, established in 2023. Situated in an orchard, it is a celebration of regenerative farming, honest winemaking, and community; in its first year it lured some titanic names in the industry.

Wine-growers to try: Domaine la Calmette (Cahors, France) and François Saint-Lô (Loire, France), Strekov 1075 (Slovakia), Dario Prinčič (Friuli-Venezia Giulia, Italy), Averill Creek and Thorn & Burrow (British Columbia, Canada), Kindeli Wines (Nelson, New Zealand).

September
Ricci Weekender, Sicily, Italy
@ricciweekender

While the rest of the Northern Hemisphere's wine-growers toil away in their cellars in September, Sicilians do what they do best – throw a wine and food showdown for the ages. Organized by DJ Giles Pederson and chef Ed Wilson, this brings together music, a load of very talented chefs, and some of Sicily's best natural wine bottles, which have in the past included Vino di Anna, Alessandro Viola, and Nino Barraco.

Wine-growers to try: Vino di Anna, Alessandro Viola, and Nino Barraco (Sicily, Italy).

October
Vini Di Vignaioli, Parma, Italy
@vinidivignaioli

A small, but perfectly formed gathering of some of Italy's most progressive winemakers, set in the soft rolling landscape outside of Parma. Being in Emilia-Romagna, expect some seriously decent food fare. This is the home of Parmesan, prosciutto, Bolognese and tiramisu, after all. Previous iterations have included L'Archetipo (Puglia), Foradori (Alto Adige), La Stoppa (Emilia-Romagna), and Bera Vittorio & Figli (Piedmont).

Wine-growers to try: L'Archetipo (Puglia, Italy), Foradori (Alto Adige, Italy), La Stoppa (Emilia-Romagna, Italy), Bera, Vittorio e Figli (Piedmont, Italy).

November
Karakterre, New York, US
@wearekarakterre @littlewine

Karakterre was born out of passion for wine and organic farming. Founders Marko Kovač and Niko Dukan have been involved with low-intervention wines for almost two decades and their relationship is not only with wine, but also the grower-farmers who consistently demonstrate their commitment to the natural environment. Mainly formed of Central and Eastern European growers, Karakterre brings together unique low-intervention wine-growers to showcase their work and ideas, as well as curating an important and evolving conversation on sustainability, and is supported by media partner Littlewine. Karakterre also holds an annual fair in Austria's Eisenstadt every May.

Wine-growers to try: Vinas Mora (Primošten, Croatia), Christian Tschida (Burgenland, Austria), Franz Strohmeier (Styria, Austria), Phelan Farm (California, US), Emidio Pepe (Abruzzo, Italy).

December
RAW WINE, Berlin, Germany
@rawwineBER @rawwineworld

When the rest of the world is winding down for Christmas, the tour de force that is Master of Wine Isabelle Legeron is ramping up for her final RAW fair of the year (see page 110). Set in a historic marketplace in Berlin's Kreuzberg, this brings together producers from all over the world who work organically or biodynamically with few (if any) additives. Isabelle also holds annual fairs all around the world.

Wine-growers to try: Frank Cornelissen (Sicily, Italy), Natur2Kinder (Franken, Germany), A Tribute to Grace (California, US), Bodega Murga (Valle de Pisco, Peru).

Resources

APPS
Three game-changing apps for natural wine hunters:

Raisin
@naturalwineapp
With its stripped-back interface, Raisin App is my constant source of reference when travelling, or discovering new natural wine spaces in my area. You can search by location and category, whether wine shop, wine bar, restaurant, or even winemakers nearby. Venues also have the chance to upload their wines, meaning if you like a particular wine, you can find where to buy it. All listings are scrutinized by Raisin's experts and featured venues must adhere to the rule of thirty-per-cent natural wines on their wine list (but the majority have much higher).

When Wine Tastes Best
@whenwinetastesbest
Based on Maria Thun's biodynamic calendar, this app is a calendar for wine-drinkers, allowing users to identify optimum days for sipping wines according to the cosmos. Ever wonder why the same wine tastes amazing on one day, and a little flat when you taste it again? Chances are it's a root day.

Littlewine
@littlewine.io
This is the world's winemaker-led knowledge platform. Wine professionals and wine-lovers can subscribe to the platform to access information directly from winemakers, including data on their wines and their vineyards, as well as general educational material on wine regions, grape varieties, agriculture, and more. (See also page 73).

Further resources

WEBSITES

Wineanorak
Global wine journal
wineanorak.com

Littlewine
The world's winemaker-led knowledge platform
www.littlewine.io

Not Drinking Poison
Natural wine culture by Aaron Ayscough
notdrinkingpoison.substack.com

The Feiring Line
Natural wine newsletter by Alice Feiring
thefeiringline.com

COURSES

A Thousand Decisions
@athousanddecisions
Hosted quarterly by ex-Ottolenghi Wine Buyer Heidi
Nam Knedsen in London, 'A Thousand Decisions' is a
four-week course covering everything you need to know
about natural wine. It begins with a history of farming
and a look at organic, biodynamic, regenerative, and
natural methods, alongside how terroir factors and
farming methods impact the soil and, ultimately the
wine in your glass.

BOOKS

Alice Feiring, *Naked Wine* (Da Capo Press, 2011)

Alice Feiring, *For the Love of Wine* (Potomac Books, 2016)

Alice Feiring, *Natural Wine for the People* (Ten Speed Press, 2019)

Alice Feiring, *To Fall in Love, Drink This* (Scribner, 2022)

Aaron Ayscough, *The World of Natural Wine* (Artisan, 2022)

Eric Asimov, *How to Love Wine* (Morrow, 2014)

Isabel Legeron, *Natural Wine* (CICO Books, 2020)

Jamie Goode, *Regenerative Viticulture* (self-published, 2022)

Jamie Goode, *The New Viticulture* (Flavour Press, 2023)

Kermit Lynch, *Adventures on the Wine Route* (Farrar Straus and Giroux, 1988).

Maria Thun, *The Maria Thun Biodynamic Calendar* (Floris Books, published yearly).

Masanobu Fukuoka, *The One-Straw Revolution* (Rodale Press, 1978)

Rachel Signer, *You Had Me at Pét-Nat* (Hachette Books, 2021

Simon J Woolf, *Amber Revolution* (Interlink Books, 2021)

References and picture credits

References

6: Preface
Excerpt from *Moon and Sun: Rumi's Rubaiyat*, translated by Zara Houshmand

26: Wine bottle illustrations inspired by the following labels: Jean-Marc Dreyer Origin Gewürztraminer Macération; Ezo Alain Castex Les Vins De Cabanon; Renaud Bruyère and Adeline Houillon Arbois Pupillin Ploussard; Imanol Garay La Altannativa

38–39: Regenerative farming
Jamie Goode, *Regenerative Viticulture* (self-published, 2022)
Masanobu Fukuoka, *The One-Straw Revolution* (Rodale Press, 1978)

29: Conventional wine-growing
J. Aubertot et al., "Pesticides, agriculture et environnement. Réduire l'utilisation des pesticides et limiter leurs impacts environnementaux", *Expertise scientifique collective, INRA/ Cemagref*, 2005

32: Organic wine-growing
The OIV, Organic viticulture is gaining terrain, *International Organisiation of Vine and Wine*, 28 Sep 2021, www.oiv.int/organic-viticulture-is-gaining-terrain

Picture credits

Index

Acknowledgements

A short yet very heartfelt thanks to a few people who have been instrumental in helping this book come to life.

To my publishers at Pavilion, Harper Collins. To Hannah Crosbie for inviting me on a podcast that would lead to the invitation to write this book (via DM, no less).

To those in my orbit who have undertaken the (almost priceless) task of looking after Leonard while I write: Mum, Dad, Aman, Karampreet, Ted and Mandi, and John, this book would not exist without you. Thank you; I love you.

To my colleagues and friends who have cheered me on and steadied me through my trembles: Ania, Jamie, Phoebe, Immy, Ellen, Abbie, Sarah, Esme, Smillet, Aidan, Kate, Louie, Tegan, Jax, Zayd, Georgia, and brilliant sister Miriam. I am so lucky to have you.

To Zoë and Layo Paskin for your support in all I do.

To those profiled in the pages of this book: Isabelle, Stefano, Mon and Tim, Keti, Christina, Sophie, Steph and Eduard, Meli, Sonia, Gina, Mees, Eddie, Doug, Margaux, Luca and Fleur. Thank you for being a part of it, I am so very grateful.

To my Danish family at Rosforth & Rosforth and biggest inspirations: Sune, Henrik, Benny, and Alex, without whom I would never have experienced such joy and adventure over a decade of discovering natural wine.

To all the vignerons who continue to blow my mind with wines so full of soul and vigour – which have energized my career and continue to imbue me with such courage and delight.

And finally, to my husband, Charlie. I love you more than I have ever found a way to say.

ACKNOWLEDGEMENTS

About the author

The rise of Honey Spencer in the world of wine has been an energetic and dynamic one so far. Her professional journey started at Jamie Oliver's Fifteen restaurant and has taken her around the world from London's Sager + Wilde, to Den Vandrette in Copenhagen, 10 William St in Sydney, and noma Mexico.

She is currently wine director for Paskin & Associates, curating the wine lists for all their acclaimed venues: The Palomar, The Barbary, The Mulwray, and one-Michelin-star Evelyn's Table. She also works as a wine consultant and has written wine lists for Glastonbury Festival's Camp Kerala, one-Michelin-star Osip in Somerset, Akoko, Bossa, and Native in London, plus Gleneagles Townhouse, Edinburgh. She has also recently opened her own restaurant Sune on Hackney's Broadway Market in London, with husband Charlie.

It is no coincidence that Honey's career has followed a similar trajectory to the popularity of natural wine with consumers; she has undoubtedly been a key player in bringing them onto the world stage. Her passion for wine and fierce pursuit of knowledge are instantly infectious. She is listed in *The Drinks Business* '50 Most Powerful Sommeliers in London' and Code's '100 Most Influential Women in Hospitality 2022', and sits on the judging panels for both the GQ Food & Drink Awards and the Fortnum & Mason Food and Drink Awards.

Whenever Honey isn't visiting wine-growers or working restaurant service, she can be found at home in a converted pub in East London with her husband, her son Len, and a table full of friends.

ABOUT THE AUTHOR

First Published in the United Kingdom in 2024 by
Pavilion
An imprint of HarperCollins*Publishers*
1 London Bridge Street
London SE1 9GF

www.harpercollins.co.uk

HarperCollins*Publishers*
Macken House
39/40 Mayor Street Upper
Dublin 1
D01 C9W8
Ireland

10 9 8 7 6 5 4 3 2 1

First published in Great Britain by Pavilion
An imprint of HarperCollins*Publishers* 2024

ISBN 978-0-00-861015-9

This book is produced from independently certified FSC™ paper
to ensure responsible forest management.

For more information visit: www.harpercollins.co.uk/green

Publishing Director: Stephanie Milner
Commissioning Editors: Kiron Gill, Lucy Smith
Copyeditor: Hilary Lumsden
Editorial Assistant: Shamar Gunning
Design Manager: Laura Russell
Senior Designer: Alice Kennedy-Owen
Designer: maru studio G.K.
Production Controller: Grace O'Byrne
Proofreader: Sue Morony
Indexer: Ruth Ellis
Illustrated by: Max Ososki

Printed and bound in China by RR Donnelley APS